By the Lake of Sleeping Children

Advance Praise for *By the Lake of Sleeping Children*

"Cool, tense, and terrifying. Sounds and sights crowd Urrea's sentences to the point that his book almost breathes. His vision of Tijuana as a garbage dump where the Third World antagonizes the First, a war zone where nothing is authentic except a word processor, is hypnotizing."
    —ILAN STAVANS, author of *The Mexican Condition*

"Read it and you will understand more than the governments and politicians. We are fortunate to have Luis Urrea, a man who loves his country. Both of them."
    —CHARLES BOWDEN, author of *Blood Orchid: An Unnatural History of America* and *Desierto: Memories of the Future*

"*By the Lake of Sleeping Children* is a splendid book—full of humor as well as important insights into the future along the Mexican–U.S. border."
    —LESLIE MARMON SILKO, author of *Ceremony* and *Yellow Woman and a Beauty of the Spirit*

"Unabashedly one-sided, stubborn in his missionary's view of the world, a literary kamikaze fusing death and sex and God and politics, Urrea's voice is worth more than all the newspaper dispatches ever written about the border for the 'objective' press."
    —RUBÉN MARTINEZ, author of *The Other Side: Notes from the New L.A., Mexico City and Beyond*

"Urrea has written a lyrical and lucid work of art. His writing is precise, clear, compassionate, and he tells a story all of North America needs to hear. I will always be grateful it was written."
    —BENJAMIN ALIRE SÁENZ, author of *Carry Me Like Water*

By the Lake

ANCHOR BOOKS
DOUBLEDAY
New York   London   Toronto   Sydney   Auckland

Luis Alberto Urrea

Photographs by John Lueders-Booth

of Sleeping

Children

The Secret Life
of the Mexican Border

AN ANCHOR BOOK
PUBLISHED BY DOUBLEDAY
a division of Bantam Doubleday Dell Publishing Group, Inc.
1540 Broadway, New York, New York 10036

ANCHOR BOOKS, DOUBLEDAY, and the portrayal of an anchor
are trademarks of Doubleday, a division of Bantam Doubleday Dell
Publishing Group, Inc.

Library of Congress Cataloging-in-Publication Data

Urrea, Luis Alberto.
　By the lake of sleeping children: the secret life of the Mexican
border / Luis Alberto Urrea; photographs by John Lueders-Booth.
　　p.　cm.
　　1. Tijuana (Baja California, Mexico)—Social conditions.
2. Mexican-American Border Region—Social conditions.
3. Ragpickers—Mexico—Tijuana (Baja California)　I. Title.
HN120.T52U773　1996
306′.09722—dc20　96-11784
CIP

ISBN 0-385-48419-4

For Joe Urrea Leyvas
    primo y
    hermano,

and for his family,
    Evelyn,
    Lisa, and
    Jessica

Carmen, Carmen,
    mi Carmen

Contents

In Mexico, nothing happens until it happens.
—Presidente de México, General PORFIRIO DÍAZ

Real heroism lies, as it always will, not in conformity or even patriotism but in acts of solitary moral courage. Which, come to think of it, is what we used to admire in our Christian savior.
—JOHN LE CARRÉ

God wouldn't have much fun in the brave new world.
—BURNING WATER

Acknowledgments

Gracias, Carmen Galicia Zazueta: my lifeline and my muse. Mother of many of these essays, and *mi doctora*. At last, because of you, I understand grace, forgiveness, and faith.

Several portions of this book first appeared in the following publications: the *San Diego Reader*—thanks, Jim Holman and Judith Moore; *DoubleTake*—thanks, Liz Phillips; the *Tucson Weekly*—thanks, Dan Huff and Doug Biggers; *The Late Great Mexican Border*—thanks, Bobby and Lee Byrd; *Many Mountains Moving*—thanks, Naomi Horii.

This book was composed in Tucson, Arizona, in an old-barrio adobe through fire, flood, plagues of locusts, and visitations of evil spirits. I owe thanks to too many *Tucsonenses* to name here for support and free tamales. A few names must be mentioned, however. First, thanks to family: to my cousin, medicine woman, and soul sister, Esperanza Urrea, and her family; and to cousin and brother, Joe Urrea, and his family. And to friends: to Chuck Bowden, thanks for your sterling advice ("Finish your book, damn it!"); to Demetria Martinez, occasional companion on the road, in madness, and onstage; to Sue Myal at Fiesta Publications for her generous support; to Laurie Ramzel, who got me to the hospital in time; to Snappy, Frances Shoberg, and all the fine people at the Cup; to Tom Miller and Brian Laird. For her kindness, warmth, and faith, I must give thanks to Glorious Gloria Chivers at the Book Mark—you inspire me at every turn. Tucson's writers owe you their eternal loyalty.

And, especially, thanks to Greg McNamee and his wife, Melissa McCormick—faithful friends, coconspirators, and fellow survivors of the Snuckles Factor. *Dominación Mundial, S.A.*

In Mexico City, thanks to Ignacio Gómez-Palacio and his family; thanks to the staff of *La Jornada*—Carmen Lira, Blanche Petrich, and José Agustín Ortiz Pinchetti; and a special *gracias* to Homero Aridjis.

Judi Mills—you are holy; the truth of this story lives in you. As ever, thanks to Jack Booth and his ravenous cameras. And I must again thank Pastor Von—you taught me more than I'll ever need to know about bravery, dignity, and dedication. You have been, and will always be, my hero. *Y Gracias a Negra y su familia*, again and always.

Several out-of-towners influenced this text in direct or indirect ways: Joanna Hurley of Santa Fe; César A. González-T.; the Desert Queens of San Diego—Twanna, Darcy, Barbara, and especially Jonna Faulkner; Gary Holthaus; Sharon Connors; Sandra Cisneros and Josie Garza *y las Santas Pecadoras of San Anto*. Thank you, Linda Hogan. And *un abrazo* for Terry Tempest Williams.

Thanks to Donella Coffey, at *Picket Fences*; Roberto Lovenheim, Paris expat; Patty Limerick and the Center for the American West; John Nichols, for efforts above and beyond; Mary Willix; Jan Bersin (Heitz); Denise Coté; and Nicki Sullivan, who came through in a dark hour.

For desert mysteries, midnights under the comet, and new dreams, to Natalie Sudman and Terri Warpinski—*lindas amigas*.

And, of course, thanks to Tony Delcavo and Pam Moser, of Bella Luna Books, Highlands Ranch, Colorado.

Finally, thanks and praise to you, Teresita Urrea, La Santa de Cabora.

Introductory Matters: Home of the Brave

The illegal immigrant is the bravest among us. The most modern among us. The prophet. . . . The peasant knows the reality of our world decades before the California suburbanite will ever get the point.
—RICHARD RODRIGUEZ

Who are they? How do they live? Why do they come?

One

I was born an American citizen in a small clinic upstairs from a Mexican drugstore near "taco row" in Tijuana, not five blocks from the old municipal bullring. I have blue eyes, spoke Spanish before I spoke English, grew up in a mix of colonia, barrio, ghetto, and suburb. My dad was a blond Mexican, late of the presidential staff, a secret-police officer, an army captain, holder of a badge of the dreaded federal judicial branch of Mexican law enforcement. The peculiarities of being a Mexican in California reduced him to working in bowling alleys until his death.

My mother was a socialite from Manhattan who had recently returned from being seriously wounded in World War II, a Red Cross front-line doughnut-and-coffee "girl" who entered Buchenwald with the GIs and in some ways never came out. She met my father in San Francisco, amid a swirl of bohemians, and love duped her into marrying Tijuana. From white gloves and demitasse cups to a dirt street and outhouses; from elegant chatter and Tiffany jewelry to a cesarean-section delivery of me, with scalpels decontaminated by being set on fire in a tray beside her bed. The peculiarities of being a widow of Tijuana left her lonely and confused until her death.

My father raised me to be 100 percent Mexican, often refusing to speak English to me, tirelessly patrolling the borders of my language, watching for any error in diction, inflection, grammar, or accent. And my mother raised me to be 100 percent American: she never spoke Spanish, and she never pronounced my name correctly once in my entire life. To her, I was Lewis. If, as some have suggested lately, I am some sort of "voice of the border," it is because the border runs down the middle of me. I have a barbed-wire fence neatly bisecting my heart.

I was the first of the immediate family to graduate from college. Instead of becoming a famous writer as I had intended, however, I spent most of a decade working in the Mexican borderlands, feeding the poor and bathing the feet of beggars. In some ways, it was a homecoming. In a dark hour, when I knew I could not continue, I was delivered by Lowry Pei and Richard Marius at Harvard. I flew away from a Baja California orphanage one June day and landed in Massachusetts, where I taught expository writing and wandered around the Yard, drunk on green trees and ivy.

I did not *immigrate*; I was already an American citizen. Besides, how can one *immigrate* from America to America?

My first home, where I stumbled into life and first greeted the astonishment of daylight, was on a hill above Tijuana. The house to the east was already giving way to gravity on the day I was born: it slumped downhill, a wooden trapezoid rushing slowly into the dry arroyo beneath our yards. In the shadow of this woozy building, bananas and pomegranates grew. The poor boys and I scrabbled in the dirt and grit of our street, throwing wooden tops to spin in the dust, herding amazingly huge red ants and pillbugs back and forth between the stones, and ambushing each other with bright pink and yellow squirt guns bought at the corner *botica* for the change left over from the kilo of tortillas we were sent to buy each afternoon.

And today, these many years later, the house next door has settled like a deck of weathered cards. The banana trees are dead and gone. Little boys like me, however, still play on the hillside. These boys have seen things that we did not even dream of. They have watched Desert Storm, Waco, Beirut, Panama, Rwanda, Bosnia, Colosio, the assassination of the Mexican bishop, Israel's *intifada*, Rodney King, the L.A. riots, Oklahoma City, the Chiapas revolt, the Million Man March, the white Ford Bronco, even the autopsy of a reported UFO pilot—all on *gringo* television, spilling south over the edges of the border as Tijuana's sewage rushes north.

The squirt guns are more expensive, and most of the boys are still poor. Creative, as the poor tend to be, they use scrap wood to form faux Uzis and Mac-10s. And some of these children have fashioned rocket launchers and mortars out of cardboard tubes. They aim at the Border Patrol helicopters swarming the fence a few miles away. Or they aim at that gleaming city on the sparkling bay. They imagine a brilliant screaming arc: copper and gold rockets raining down on the border, vivid explosions among the banks, the hotels, the traffic, the bistros, the airports of San Diego, California. Ten freeway miles away. One hundred years as the crow flies.

Lately, young Mexican intellectuals with a slightly revolutionary bent have coined a pet name for Tijuana. They call it *Palestijuas*, Tijuana-Palestine. I look up at that old hill and realize that my own grandma's house is in the dead heart of tomorrow's Golan Heights.

This is . . . a tale of two cities. Each of the city's metropolitan areas houses about one million people. One city is geographically small and the people live in close proximity. One city is large and sprawling.

In one city, inhabitants still suffer diseases considered exotic in the other: cholera, polio, typhus, tuberculosis, rickets. In the other city, separated from the former mostly by an imaginary line, lies some of the richest real estate in the richest half of the richest state in the richest country on the face of the earth.

—JOSEPH WAMBAUGH, *Lines and Shadows*

We were not, in the sense of the people you will meet in this book, *poor*. I was, compared to my cohorts at Harvard, however, a pauper. It's all a matter of perspective—as is the Tijuana municipal garbage dump. Still, in my first years of life, I survived scarlatina, German measles, skin diseases, chronic coughs, diarrhea, and tuberculosis. It is still 1896 in Tijuana. And it is also 2025.

I learned something at Harvard, though, and I hope you will carry it with you as you read this book. Everyone, no matter who, no matter how rich or poor, has lived in the Tijuana garbage dump. One's type of suffering does not rate, in my book, above or below anyone else's. You can be as impoverished as a trash-picker driving your 240 SL down the Garden State Parkway to your yacht at Cape May. We are all equal under this particular sun.

The only difference is, the suffering suburbanite is probably not hungry, ill, in constant danger, or watching babies die. The suburbanite is not being chased by helicopters. The 240 SL is not a dirt-floored shack with no heat, no water, no electricity, no furniture, no plumbing, no appliances, no bed, no blankets, no rugs, no stove.

Border Patrol Moves to Fire 5 for Misconduct

Inquiry: Agents hit illegal immigrants with rock, then covered up the incident. Agency says it's sending a message.
—*Los Angeles Times*, October 24, 1995

Messages are illegal immigrants, too. Along with ideas, language, and culture. Things shift. Things change. News travels fast.

Someone I know gets in touch with me and tells me, "Listen to this. Tijuana's murder rate is roughly 10 percent of San Diego's. It's in the paper. Equal populations—Tijuana could even be *bigger* than San Diego. Who can count? Who can get in all those canyons and really count? But imagine it, old evil Tijuana, old Calcutta of the West, statistically proven to be over 90 percent safer than San Diego, California. Don't you just love it?"

I love it.

A few years ago, I wrote a book called *Across the Wire*. I didn't know it at the time, but that book was to be the first volume of a series, of which this is the second installment. It was based partly on those wild years of working with the missionaries and relief guerrillas of Spectrum Ministries Inc., under the command of the incomparable Pastor Von; and it was partly a selection of my dispatches written for my job as nightmare correspondent for an alternative weekly newspaper.

Since then, people get in touch with me. Some of them want to go to Tijuana, to work with Von, to look around, to write an article or a book, to do graduate research, or to do a television or radio show. Very few want to send money. A couple of them, for a very short time, wanted to film a movie.

This was the pitch: "Tijuana's foxiest female detective is investigating a gruesome series of serial killings. The killings take place in the garbage dumps. However, this woman is from the upper classes—she doesn't know her own lower class. The only way she can get into the subculture is to hook up with renegade Pastor Von. He, of course, is the rugged missionary who works with the Mexicans. Okay? Now, in the course of the investigation, she finds a spiritual awakening, sure, but she also has a *torrid affair with Von!* Big chase in the trash, you know, tractors, fire, the whole nine yards."

Tijuana's foxiest detective?

Although Clint Eastwood would have made a perfect Pastor Von, plugging malefactors with a .44 Mag in one hand and saving the foxy detective with the Bible in his other, and although I would have loved to roll around in a really big pile of money, I could not say yes.

ACROSS THE WIRE II: BIBLE STUDY OF BLOOD
Von's back—and he's pissed! They pushed him too
far this time, and now it's PERSONAL. Heathens diss
Jesus . . . and Von sends 'em to Hell in a Frenzy of
"Righteous Wrath"!
Pray to God he doesn't come gunning for YOU!

A lot has happened to the border since I wrote that modest little volume. NAFTA, for example; the astonishing Proposition 187; the rise of PAN and breakaway political movements; the surge in drug cartel shenanigans; the advent of Tijuana's spit-and-polish border cops, the Beta Group; various executions and shootouts; border closings, new fences, interdiction programs; amazing floods that ravaged downtown Tijuana and left over a million tons of mud in the streets; a savage drought; California's mini-depression; tourist-gobbling human-sacrifice *santería* cult drug gangs; rumors of Border Patrol ID computer chips to be inserted under the skin on the foreheads of Mexicans and gringos, electronically telling roving satellites which is which; the financial near-collapse of Mexico and the disgrace and exile of the "reform president," Salinas de Gortari.

Tijuana is no longer the city it was in 1993. Of course, anyone who knows anything about the border can tell you that Mexican border towns change radically every twenty-four hours, yet never have—and never will—change. Tijuana, Tecate, Mexicali, Nogales, Nuevo Laredo, Ciudad Juárez, Reynosa, Matamoros, and their various sisters are cities-as-Zen-koans.

Tijuana *is* the sound of one hand clapping.

In the barrios in and around Tijuana, it is not uncommon to hear such comments as "I'm afraid to go across the border. They're crazy up there!" Tijuana, after all, has a positively genteel murder rate compared to ours. A Mexican visitor told me, "The Americans have no culture. They have no way of life!"

So if it's so bad here, why are they coming?

Because we have money.

Not only do we have money, but we live in Disneyland, where we spend large bagfuls of that money. We also enjoy good booze, lots of sex, we get to shoot everybody we don't like, we drive shiny cars really fast and occasionally jump them through burning buildings or over police barricades, we exercise on big machines that look like UFOs, and we love Jesus. We are proud of these facts, and we advertise them twenty-four hours a day, all over the world.

Television, radio, movies, and recordings invite visitors

from all over the world to visit the Magic Kingdom © (R) (Pat. Pend.).

Our ambassadors wave and smile and say, Come on and get some! Starsky and Hutch, Mickey Mouse, Madonna, those buff lifeguards on *Baywatch*, Michael Jackson, Sharon Stone, Beavis and Butt-Head, the Roadrunner, Gloria Estefan, Indiana Jones: Come on down!

Fortunately for the Mexicans, they live right outside the back fence of Fantasyland. And as everyone knows, Fantasyland is a few short steps away from Tomorrowland.

We have fabulous rides: elevators, escalators, sidewalks, bays, beaches, parks, buses, bicycles, cars, jets. We have food. We have such awesome exhibits as the lawn, the swimming pool, the Safeway supermarket, the bikini, the superbra, neon signs, Las Vegas, garbage trucks. We have pet food! We have the amazing flush toilet. We have Kotex, sprinklers, floors, canned frijoles, Twinkies, Hulk Hogan, *Playboy*, three-ply scented toilet paper, roach motels, lowriders, der Wienerschnitzel, glass windows, MTV, and death-metal. Batman, Steven Seagal, Sly Stallone, and those brave Cartwright boys from the Ponderosa Ranch patrol the streets, keeping order. We have hospitals, emergency rooms, dentists, and Slurpees.

Yes, we even have that amazing ride called welfare.

We do not have death squads, torture chambers, the "dirty war," famine, civil war, guerrillas, CIA advisers, cartels, or "the disappeared." Yet.

Night and day, the hungry watch us frolic in Disneyland. The lights are always on. They can see the glow reflected on the poison clouds of pollution. They see the ads on TV. They want to come in and ride.

Oh, and there's one other thing—if they don't get in the

gates, their babies might very well die of starvation, disease, or misadventure. What choice would you make?

> Americans spend more than $4 billion each year on pet food. That's four times more than they spend on food to aid all the hungry nations of the world; it's five times more than they spend on research into the causes of cancer; it's nine times more than the American Heart Association has spent since its inception, 33 years ago.
> —CAROLINE KNAPP, *Boston Phoenix*, October 9, 1984

We Americans can't seem to agree on anything. (We Mexicans can't either.) Rush Limbaugh and Hillary Clinton are never going to dance a waltz together. Yet there is one subject on which Republicans and Democrats have reached a consensus: if those _____ [insert any "Third World" people here] can't feed their babies, then they should stop having them. (Have you ever noticed that no politician ever said, "Damn it, those Norwegians have just got to stop reproducing"?)

I wonder, once we Hispanics have taken over the United States and it is utterly browned (to use the new, semi-nauseating p.c. phrase—sounds like something you get out with bleach), will Swedes and Icelanders suddenly swarm our shores, float in on inner-tube rafts? Will 1,200 new Serb-speaking Chicano officers be added to the Border Patrol? Will wily Nuyorican INS agents root out illegal Canadians by listening to lunchtime conversations to hear if anyone says, "Eh?"

On the surface of it, the baby issue seems to make perfect sense. There are too many of you: like an overpopulated elk herd, you're starving; like the desperate elk, you are migrating into our territory; you're eating our forage, bringing new ticks and tapeworms from your feeding grounds, and you're generally dirtying up our sparkly gene pool. So stop it. Take these pills, roll these nice condoms over your members, pop this little diaphragm over your cervix, tie those pesky tubes, give it a rest, put a cork in it, cross your legs, tie it in a knot, and die off a little.

By the way, it doesn't matter that you were here first.

The feature we fail to understand is that, in Mexico at least, these poorest of people have no welfare, no retirement funds, no safety net, no savings, no money, no health insurance, no life insurance, no social security, no unemployment benefits, no workers' comp. Other Mexicans ostensibly receive social security coverage from birth to death, but these are a stratum beneath the bottom.

The mortality rate among children is high. New afflictions arrive every year—recent hurricanes that raked Mexico over and over; earthquakes; droughts; that baffling plague called AIDS (SIDA in Mexico); killer bees; now a swarm of super-mosquitoes, furious little ICBMs spiraling out of the south, bearing new and hardy waves of old killers, poxes and dengues that nobody can cure; a terrifying disease that is crawling north and is called "the evil fever"; *maquiladora* diseases along the border, strange PCB and mercury and radium buds that bloom in wombs and spinal columns.

Mamá and Papá, just like Mom and Pop, worry about the future.

And in spite of populist propaganda on posters glued by the ton to lightpoles and walls all over Mexico—posters that the peasants can't read—the man in the street knows that the situation is getting worse. It is not a theory or a queasy feeling in his gut as he scans the *Wall Street Journal*. He cannot afford the tortillas to feed his children.

His solution, so baffling to rational gringos, is simple: have more children.

Why? Because children *are* insurance; children *are* social security. Children were once this country's social security as well, you might recall. We had kids, sent them to school, gave them a little money, maybe the family business, and they would watch out for us in our old age. Weren't we surprised when they shipped us off to old folks' homes and "supervised care" feedlots?

You're a garbage-picker in the Tijuana dump. You have eight babies. Four die. Four grow up. Those four are bound by family ties, religion, cultural mores to care for you. Even if one of them becomes a drunk (many do, and who can blame them), three are working. That's six strong arms—added to Mamá and Papá, ten strong arms. Already they're a small corporation. If Papá gets ill, as he often does, gets killed, as he often does, gets drunk and runs off with la Pancha from the hut next door, as he has been known to do, or if *el norte* calls him and he vanishes through the fence, as we know all too well he is wont to do, that leaves eight strong arms, and built-in bodyguards and providers for lonesome Mamá.

Time rolls on. Those three kids get married and have their own kids. The wives and the new kids also look out for you. You, in turn, teach the kids things, babysit, provide moral guidance, and often tend to the homestead. You get too old for the heavy work, but you can sweep, change diapers, get goodies from the missionaries, cook, lie to the cops, keep the thieves and addicts out of the house, kill chickens, slop hogs, take your few coins to the store and buy a can of Carnation milk. In family matters, you are the judge. When a spanking is due, you are the executioner. When history, tradition, *continuity* are needed, you are the icon.

The equation could not be simpler: more children=more chances to survive.

How can you convince a trash-picker of the other equation that so worries us today: more people=the end of the world?

Although the myth of Tijuana is that it is a teeming staging area for a massive assault on America, you might be surprised at how many people have no intention of ever crossing the border. No matter what anyone tells you, a population of more than a million people, living in one of the top money-making cities in Mexico, and the most visited city, and the most reviled city, and the most Disneyfied city, are not going to crunch through the fabulous fence we have erected. They aren't going anywhere.

But their children might.

Wouldn't you? If we are honest about this, we have to admit there is simply no question. It would be "Pack your duffel, Buffy—we're off to Orange County!" The various enraged golfers and hausfraus with their BUFFY GO HOME signs wouldn't faze you one bit.

Borders dissolve all over the globe, and nobody knows what to do about it.

A group of German delegates attending a multinational conference on immigration in San Diego was taken to the new stretch of fence along the border. They peered through the fence at the Mexicans peering back at them. The hosts, various well-meaning Saviors of the American Way, thought the practical Germans would be impressed with the brilliant engineering of the fence. Imagine their alarm when the TV cameras went on and the German spokesman, visibly distressed, turned away from the border and said into the mike, "We tore down *our* wall," and walked away.

□ □ □ □

In all the border talk, there is one ugly fact that nobody wants to admit: the border crossings are not going to stop, because neither government wants them to stop.

If the American government really wanted to stop the crossings, the border would be sealed as tight as an envelope. Small "triumphs" are allowed—El Paso and Juárez have new fences and patrols and bottlenecks and no illegals. Shazam! That's, what, five miles out of two thousand. Your tax dollars at work.

I wonder if the Border Patrol ever feels betrayed.

Do you like lettuce? How about tomatoes? Onions. Garlic. Peaches. Avocados. Cotton.

Sugar.

Oranges. Apples. Cherries. Cabbage. Cauliflower. Asparagus. Grapes. Pecans. Walnuts. Pumpkins.

And you don't want to spend $15.00 for a quart of strawberries or $5.30 for a can of peas. How about $20.98 for a pair of Jockey shorts?

It's called agribusiness, multinational free enterprise, and if for no other reason than that, the border will never be closed. Unless, of course, U.S. citizens suddenly develop strong backs again, and a ferocious work ethic, and brave, very brave, hearts. Lately I haven't seen lines of Harvard grads or third-generation welfare recipients in the four A.M. dusk in Phoenix or Blythe or Bakersfield, where the buses collect people and haul them out into the brutal sun.

The drug war? Venture capitalism at its best. Supply and demand. And peasants grow it, harvest it, mule it across the border, and do the fine corporate service of catching lots of those flying bullets that could really slow down business at the home office.

Imagine a closed border. Instant Mexican revolution! What then? What would happen to the American Way of Life with a burning two-thousand-mile-long back porch? How many untold millions of refugees would then cross the border? How long until outside assistance would be sought by one side or the other? How long until we were forced into the battle? What would it be like if the cardboard rocket launchers in my old Tijuana colonia suddenly became real? Below Mexico, Central America is as dry as San Diego's chaparral, and people there are eager for a good-sized match to fly down and ignite them. Smoke from Hollywood to Medellín.

Carter knew it. Reagan knew it. Bush knew it. Clinton knows it. Even Newt, Pete Wilson, Teddy Kennedy, and Rush know it.

Consider the 1996 election-year sabre rattling of the Clinton White House—Troops on the Border. There are bold threats to seal the whole thing, posting Guardsmen and other soldiers along the fence, intensifying the tech-war with new sensors and light towers, beefing up the walls and fences, hiring more Border Patrol agents. The limited program has a stunning effect in California and Arizona. However, it has an even more stunning effect in Mexico City, where such threats of a closed border are taken very seriously indeed.

Within days of Janet Reno's early January announcement that the border would be militarized, emergency sessions of the cabinet of Mexico's Secretary of the Interior were called. On Friday, January 12, the Mexican government was considering a petition for United Nations troops to patrol their side of the line, thus ensuring the safety of Mexican nationals. It seems to be a right-wing militia and Freeman's fondest nightmare come true.

Within three weeks of the small-scale closing of the borders, reports appeared in the Mexican media showing the increasing crisis on the Mexican side of the border, as the tension was already starting to grow intolerable. Dread, drought, and the depression were aggravated by the trapped humans waiting to run. On the United States side, reports showed increased arrests, beefed-up high-tech equipment, and the mighty computerized fingerprinting program that will cull even more illegals. Shops and stores in San Ysidro, California, and Nogales, Arizona, immediately reported heavy losses in sales, layoffs, and closings. The Mexicans called more sessions. And those sincere politicians in Washington hoped lots of gringos would rush out and vote for the newly engineered tough-on-beaners president.

What, in all this hand-wringing and chest-thumping, really happened? About three hundred troops were sprinkled upon the border like Sweet 'n Low. Roughly three fourths of one troop per every ten miles of border. San Diego and Tucson. And already, the smoke of a smoldering Mexico started rising.

When a politician in San Diego suggested that land mines along the border would be a good option, Mexico immediately joked that they'd disarm the mines and sell them at the swap meet. When Pat Buchanan suggested that we erect a Great Wall of China all along the border, Mexicans circulated jokes to the effect that Mexican workers would be building the wall, anyway. They'd still make money. Then, when the wall was complete, Mexicans all along the line could set up photo booths where they could charge gringo tourists to pose for a portrait by the wall. And, later, when border perestroika kicked in, the Mexicans would be hired to tear it all back down.

Can the Mexican border be sealed? Is there some hermetic lock the politicians can put on two thousand miles of mostly wasteland and desert? And if they do, who will be the scapegoat then?

Watch for the rising smoke.

□ □ □ □

But let's keep our minds on that can of peas.

I am not condemning the system—I like cheeseburgers and creamed corn as much as the next guy. But I hear these things everyone is saying about my cousins: "Illegals are costing us money. They get free benefits. They have babies in our hospitals. They are sneaking in and trying to make their children *Americans.*"

True enough. I can live with that until some new, better scapegoat comes along. But I would like to say one small thing on their behalf. They are trying to bring the United States the best they have to offer. They come here not to have babies, though they'd be fools to miss the opportunity. They come here not to lounge around enjoying welfare benefits, though in every group there are people who make the best of a sucker-play. They come here to make their best efforts, to work—to work *hard*—to better themselves, to enjoy a better world, to get educated, and to prosper. It's the American dream writ large. They're just writing it in Spanish.

The social Darwinists in the U.S. government should appreciate the brutal winnowing process. The weak do not survive this midnight entry. Only the strong are inheriting this particular earth. As many other countries know, many "illegal immigrants" come in not to work the fields and attempt to feed the nation but to plant bombs and foment revolt. Consider Israel. Consider the contras.

The people I write about are the financial backbone of Dole, Green Giant, McDonald's, Stouffers, Burger King, the Octopus car wash chain, Del Monte, Chicken of the Sea, Heinz, Hunt's, Rosarito, Campbell's *m-m-m good*, Wendy's, Taco Bell, Lean Cuisine, Dinty Moore, Hormel, midnight shifts, front lawn raking, pool scrubbing, gas station back rooms, blue-jean stitching, TV assembly, athletic-shoe sole gluing, shit-taking, shit-scrubbing, shit-eating, bent-back silent frightened work crews everywhere. Cost-effective and the baseline upon which all these corporations build. If they weren't a well-integrated part of the machine, *they would be replaced.*

Illegals work, in every sense of the word.

Directly or indirectly, that ketchup on those potatoes with that dinner salad and those chips and salsa and that tuna sandwich and that cloth napkin and that ice-cold lemonade were all provided by the hands of the people I write about here.

How much money would you imagine that involves? Does it cover the birth of a new American citizen?

> The conservatives love their cheap labor; the liberals love their cheap cause. (Neither group, you will notice, ever invites the immigrants to move into their *homes.* Not into *their* homes!)
> —Edward Abbey

Taxes. They pay federal and state taxes—no refunds. FICA. SSI. Sales Tax. Fines. Contributions. Coins in Catholic poor boxes. Phone bills. Gas and electric bills.

Say there are over three million undocumented workers in the United States and each worker has money removed, as do we all, from his paycheck. How much money might it be? Where does that money go? On a very small scale, where does the payroll check of the deported illegal go? What of the flower ranch in an unnamed southern California county which, miraculously, suffers a Border Patrol raid on the day before the seasonal paychecks are going to be distributed? The underpants sewing factory? I can take you to the paper-walled homes of men and women just like you who have learned these vivid lessons about multinational business. They're experts.

Sales tax. Gasoline tax. Cigarette tax. Liquor tax. How much?

Gasoline, food, medicine, speeding tickets, alcohol, clothes, shoes, aspirin, used cars, English classes, community college textbooks, toothpaste, movies, used furniture, televisions, pets, pet food, underwear, pencils, gym clothes, school lunches, tampons, tobacco, bus fares, postage, hamburgers, Coca-Cola, bank accounts, credit cards, interest.

How much?

If we want to get a picture of how much these Mexican "parasites" actually contribute to the United States, we might look at what they contribute to Mexico. Douglas W. Payne, in his article "Mexico and Its Discontents," in the April 1995 *Harper's*, noted, "After all, the greatest open secret in U.S.–Mexican relations . . . is Mexico's tacit support of illegal immigration." He points out that the poor in Mexico are "dead weight." Until they come across the wire, of course, when they are transformed by the magic of Disney Imagineering into layers of golden eggs. Payne reports:

> Already an estimated 10 percent of Mexico's population, or nine to ten million Mexicans, now live in the United States, and many of them send money south. The Mexican central bank calculates that dollar remittances to Mexico top $2 billion annually; independent studies indicate that the figure is actually higher. The remittances are now the third largest source of hard currency for Mexico, after oil and tourism.

That would mean $2 billion mailed and wired to Mexico annually *after* cost-of-living money, fun money, rent money, bill-paying money, and all the other daily moneys have been spent here. That is, $2 billion is counted only from those who remit; no one knows how much is not mailed home. Let us focus on that money for a moment. How much do you send to your mom? Ten percent of your paycheck? If we stick to this overly generous figure, it tallies up to $20 billion dollars floating around the United States every year. In other words, one extra Bill Gates. It's the Mexosoft Corporation.

President Salinas de Gortari wasn't kidding when he said, "I am for the free movement of labor."

All aboard! Next stop—¡Disneylandia!

Two

I don't want to give the impression that this is a sociology text, or a political science tome, or a religious book. I don't benefit from all the schooling these subjects require. I haven't read all the books. I don't have a research grant or a database or a political theory. All I did was live there and walk the streets, bury some dead people and feed some live ones. I didn't have time to read about it. You know what the Chinese say: The bird sings not because it has an answer but because it has a song.

This is an adventure story. It's nature writing. It's a forum for the voiceless.

I have told this story before, and it bears some repeating. One day I was leaning on a missionary van, writing in my journal. The day was particularly ripe with beauty and horror. It was hot. And a man working the trash came over to me and said, "What are you doing?"

"Writing," I said. "See?" I showed him the notebook.

He couldn't read, but he squinted and looked at the words.

"What are you writing about?" he asked.

"This," I said, gesturing at the dump.

He turned and looked.

"This?" he said, astounded.

"Yes. It's a journal, you see. Like a diary."

"Wait a minute," he said. "You're writing about us."

"Yes, I am. I write down what I see, what I hear, what you do."

"You're writing about me," he said.

I nodded.

Emotions washed over his face, and some of them looked like anger. I prepared myself to get scolded. I didn't know if he'd throw a punch or walk away.

"Will people read it?" he asked.

"Someday."

He nodded, a fierce scowl on his face.

"Good," he said. "Good! You write it down. Write it all down. Because I live in the garbage, and I'll die in the garbage, and I'll be buried in the garbage. And nobody will ever know that I lived. So tell them about me. Tell them I was here."

I sit in the garage-door home of Negra (whose real name is Ana María), one of the heroes of my last Tijuana book. One of my heroes. I met her when she was a tiny barefoot girl living in the old *dompe*. She and I have grown up together in many ways—she is now a woman of twenty-five, and her children are the age she was when I first met her. Her daughter is whooping and dancing in a circle. And Negra says, "Elsa, you're dancing around like an Indian."

Negra's mother says, "She *is* an Indian!"

"Oh," Negra says.

She is ferocious. When she was seven months pregnant, she got into a scuffle with a woman down the hill, and she picked the woman up by the hair, threw her into the street, dove on her, rolling back and forth across the jagged stones and pummeling her bloody. Negra won the fight. Later she said, "I didn't like the way she was looking at me. I told her to show some respect, or I'd teach her how." A free lesson.

She has an alarming scar on her forearm. It is the size of the heel of a loaf of sourdough bread, raised and lumpy. This scar is a constant reminder of Negra's steely will. Her lover once cheated on her with a girl from the other side of the dump. In the manner of many couples in the area, he'd cajoled Negra into tattooing his name on herself, to show whose woman she was. When Negra discovered his deceit, she took a metal serving spoon and put it in the fire. When the metal was glowing, red-hot, when the little oval openings in the spoon that let the juice run out were bright rings of orange light, she put the spoon against her arm and melted his tattooed name out of her skin.

When he came home, she showed him her arm and asked if he planned to cheat on her again.

Negra is famous.

She has been on television, and she is the only person in the barrio to have her picture in a book. Brazilian reporters sit in her living room and politely refuse anything to drink. Gringos occasionally endanger her by appearing in the barrio asking after her. The neighbors are suspicious of these strangers. They gossip. And gossip can get you killed.

Although she is famous, she is not yet rich—she isn't even near escaping poverty. Gifts and hope pile up on good days. Toys from the latest radio station Christmas toy drive are still holding together, though conditions in these dirty alleys are hard on things. The dolls have a sort of leprous skin condition, their arms and legs suffering a mysterious patina of gray-brown biological smearing. All the dolls are naked. Things are looking up. Still, when I ask her what she dreams about for the future, she just stares at me.

"What?" she says.

"What are your hopes?" I say. "What do you dream of?"

"I don't understand what you're talking about," she replies.

We are about to go film a news report at the *dompe*. Negra is excited. She has put on her best shiny gold shoes.

We bang over the million stones and ruts of back-street Tijuana until we get to the dump, now an official barrio of the city, with a name and electricity and a small school provided by another border hero, David Lynch (not the movie director, but the director of a group called Responsibility). Negra shows me where they organized an Easter egg hunt last year and walks to a spot where a man was executed, or dumped after being executed elsewhere.

"He had bullets in his head," she says. "His head was all full of holes."

"How terrible," I say.

She shrugs.

"It sure ruined our egg hunt," she says.

Later she leads me back up to the hill where her uncle was burned to death by a gang of junkies. They set fire to his aluminum-siding hut, and he stayed inside. We peer into a small cement-block cube.

"This was his chimney," she says. "See that gray dust in there? See those bones?"

"I do."

"That's him." She touches a chunk of gristly bone and says, "Hello, uncle."

We find a square of ancient green shag carpeting. It stinks, and is almost too heavy to pick up. We each take a corner and pry it loose from the dirt.

"Feel this," she says. "It's full of his grease. He must have melted."

Afterward, we go to Tacos El Paisano. Negra won't eat guacamole.

"I'm on a diet," she says.

We enjoy the miraculous little *carne asada* tacos. I remember too late that I forgot to wash my hands before I ate. I have smears of Negra's uncle on my jeans.

All around the former dump, which, as a full-fledged neighborhood, just recently added phone service, are the empty shells of future *maquiladoras*. (We think our hookup charges are high. They charged Negra $500 to drop a phone line and jack into her house.) The *maquis* are waiting for NAFTA to get rolling. So far, the most obvious NAFTA action in Tijuana—still hidden from plain sight—is the purchase of the new *dompe* by Americans. The *San Diego Reader* reports the amazing news that the Texans who now run the dump plan to make $9 million a year. This figure would be so unbelievable to the garbage-pickers wandering through the heaps like droids, recycling bottles, aluminum, plastic, copper, glass, that they would laugh in your face if you told them. "The Texans," Negra says, "are good to us."

Maquis, of course, are binational or multinational factories. They sit on their bulldozed hills like raw-concrete forts, and the huts of the peasants ring their walls. Some of them have Japanese names on them, some of them have American names. All along Tijuana's new high-tech highway, el Periférico, you can see them up there, receding into the hazy distance. Headstones for the graveyard of American union labor.

Negra had a job at Imperial Toys for a while. It was a thrill—no more toil in the trash. Besides, her huge pregnant belly limited her severely in her ability to do stoop-work, although her recent triumph in street fighting lifted her morale quite a bit. At Imperial, she was earning a few cents an hour, but all she had to do was stand in one place on the assembly line. Fourteen hours a day. She was allowed two bathroom breaks, she says. She had to eat lunch standing up. When she tired, eight months pregnant now, and sat down after becoming dizzy, she was fired and thrown out.

Interestingly enough, in its rush to prepare for great profits and an industrial rebirth, Tijuana wildly bulldozed and built, scraped hilltops into canyons and threw roads and factories and warehouses and living quarters together. The utopian workers' condos at the foot of Negra's hill are now, a few years down the line, collapsing. Floors come apart and pancake down on each other. Squatters live in them, their laundry flapping out the windows like curtains. And the raw hills, left unlandscaped and unplanted, came down in the floods and swept into the city, carrying off victims, burying streets and neighborhoods, and costing unreported fortunes to clean up.

All this to tell you how things have changed in Tijuana.

I have been hanging out with Negra and her family, on and off, since 1978. Everyone knows me. The neighbors know me well enough to take things I've brought for her if she's not home. We have had neighborhood parties in her yard, dances where the tiny Indian women dig into my breastbone with their foreheads and patiently try to teach me new steps. We have had tragedies, baptisms, church services, barn-raisings, birthday dinners, piñatas, cookouts, hog sloppings, and television documentaries.

Recently, however, I drove up to her house and got out. Within five minutes a white pickup truck with three men stopped beside my Jeep. They had a clipboard. They called

her out. "Who is the gringo?" the one with the official docu-
ments demanded.

"He's my *compadre*," she said. "He looks like a gringo, but
he's a Mexican."

They had her name. The number of people living in her
house. And they demanded my name, which they wrote
down, along with the license-plate number of my car. They
stared at me for a moment, and the one with the clipboard
nodded once, his eyes completely hidden by dark glasses.
Then they sped away.

"Who's that?" I asked.

"Government agents," she replied. "The Chiapas rebels
said they were going to bring the war to the border so the
world wouldn't ignore them anymore."

"They're going to fight the Americans?" I said.

"They're going to fight Mexicans, but so the gringos can
watch. And now the Mexican government is keeping an eye
on all the Indian settlements on the border. That's who that
was."

"Are you scared?"

"Not yet."

Three

You saw how close that last election was. The country is in a
very delicate condition. They're facing some sort of revolution as their culture pulls apart. I'll say it here, now. Somebody has to say it: beef up the borders. Get new Border Patrol
agents on the line, and be ever vigilant. There will be a new
onslaught of foreign-speaking strangers that we can no longer
support. There is no more room in the lifeboat, and their

ways are not our ways. And now, with NAFTA, we have much more to lose.

New hordes of Quebecois and Canadians are going to sneak into Vermont and Maine.

Negra continues to work and raise her children. We are planning to write her autobiography someday. She wants her story told.

Pastor Von continues his superhuman efforts on the border. I occasionally run into him down there. We laugh about the old times, and young new workers hustle about, staring at me and wondering who I am and why I'm not working.

Von-watchers trade sightings of him like baseball cards. He's like a combination of Woodrow Call and Gus McRae if they were wrapped up in a single body, knew the Bible, and were Rangering for Moses.

Recently he was spotted walking into a church and looking at the uptight members of the congregation as they sat there in their suits and ties and sang bland Baptist hymns. Very few of them ever ventured into Mexico with him. Some of them would send their kids, hoping to instill some sort of missionary zeal in them, as long as Von did the dirty work for them. They turned to him with clean faces and mild smiles, awaiting a pleasant word or a blessing from the Great Man. Before he walked out, he had only one thing to say to them.

He said, "Dead sheep."

My most vivid memory of Pastor Von is one he probably doesn't recall at all. It reminds me of his delicate touch, his ability to take charge of a situation with a sophistication and spiritual wisdom that you simply can't pick up on a Sunday morning or read in a leadership book. Above all else, I see

Von as a commander. And a commander must have grace under fire.

We were in the dump—the former dump, retired and covered over now.

Von, as usual, was inside, bathing the boys. I was in charge of the clothing distribution, and I was softhearted. Being the translator, I had heard the terrible stories of at least 30 of the 150 women lined up facing me. I had seen some of them naked beside our doctors, I wiped blood off some of them or their children, I had sat in their small homes chatting about the most heinous things: rapes, stabbings, three-foot tapeworms, demons, diseases.

I didn't have the heart to be stern with them. Who was I to give them orders? Who was I to command them to line up and shut up?

They were all poor. Crushingly poor. And poverty, as I mentioned in the last book, ennobles no one. It makes women ferocious and tough, willing to do anything to get a little extra for their children or themselves.

I was being pressed into the side of the van in a cloud of human stench. The raw smell of hot women: armpits and feet, bad teeth and old clothes. And the voices pounded at me, shrill and wheedling, demanding, obscene, angry, laughing: a high-pitched babble that was making me dizzy. They were kicking up dust, so I couldn't breathe. And two of my very best friends were pressed up against me, whispering, "Save us something special" in my ears. One rubbed her arm across my crotch. The other maneuvered her breasts against me, rubbing them on my arms and my chest as she smiled up into my face. "My baby" flew at me, and "Please brother," and "You love me—forget these bitches," and "Give me some clothes now, you asshole!" Pushing, pushing, and the hands started to grab at me, fingernails clawing red welts in my skin, my glasses knocked aside, knees, kicks, slamming me back against the van, and punches started to fly, and the noise rose, and a hand closed over my privates, and another moved around my ass and squeezed as they all surged and yelled and screamed and I got hit with a leathery fist.

It was the first time I understood the saying "Seeing red."

A red sheet fell across my eyes, and I picked up the woman closest to me and threw her back into the crowd and started whipping the clothes at them, yelling back in their yelling faces. I had foolishly stirred a mini-riot into a swirling gang fight. The women who had been pressing their sexuality against me were gone in a flash, scrambling for the clothes. Dogs on the edges of the crowd went mad and started snapping and barking, attacking the fighters.

I fought my way through the women, blind in my panic and fury. I was shaking. I abandoned the dump entirely and took off cross-country. I didn't know where I was going. I was ready to walk to Mexico City if I had to.

I found myself about a half-mile away, still hearing their small voices squeaking across the land as they fought. I was standing at the side of a pigpen. I was shaking my head and crying, muttering, disoriented and scared.

Soon Von moseyed up to me and stood there, looking at the pigs. He never looked at me.

"Look at those pigs!" he said.

"Yeah."

"Did you ever see such a fat pig?"

The mother pig was indeed monumentally fat.

I shook my head.

"Look at those babies," he said.

"Yeah."

"How do they survive in there without being crushed?" he said.

"I don't know."

"Let's watch."

So we watched the massive mother walk around in the mud, knocking piglets aside. Suddenly she sat down on one, oblivious to its screeching beneath her. The little pig fought its way out from under her and turned and gave her a poisonous look, then trotted away making its *grutt-grutt-greeeet* sounds.

Von and I started laughing.

"Isn't that funny," he said.

"Yes, it is."

We stood there another minute, silent. I remember the bright gold of the grasses, the pale blue sky, the white speckles of trash that had blown away from the dump. They looked like small patches of snow, or broken pieces of clouds caught in the wild oats and foxtails.

"Feel better?" he said.

I nodded.

"Should we get back to work now?"

I nodded.

"Let's go."

He put his hand on my back and led me gently back into the dump.

I said, "Thank you, Von," but he had already gone into the bathing room. He had at least fifty more boys to wash.

The women, abashed and quiet, came to me and put their arms around me. We all stood there, under the smoke of the burning trash, hanging on to each other. We could hear the boys in the bathhouse, excitedly shouting, "Bon! Bon! Bon!"

A few words on the text.

Although in some ways this book is an update on the lives of various protagonists of *Across the Wire*, it stands alone. After that book was complete, I continued writing for the *Reader* in San Diego, and much of this collection comes from essays and reportage originally published there. Again, however, I must offer these caveats:

This book is in no way a portrait of Mexicans, Mexican culture, or "Mexicanness." It is a particular view of a particular class of people, the underdogs, *los olvidados.* As I said in the last book, it is as much an overview of Mexican life as a visit to the South Bronx is a view of Middle America.

This is not an objective document.

I am not writing, after all, about numbers, trends, units, or theories. This book is about humans. Poor humans. And it is unashamedly on their side. These are my friends, you see. We have looked into each other's eyes. We have tasted each other's lips.

"The Bald Monkey and Other Atrocities" is the one chapter in this book I would not choose to read. It deals with brutality, and it brought me my first death threats. After the *Reader* published it, I got calls from animal lovers threatening to castrate me, to cut me open and fill my body cavity with ice, and to come over and commit suicide at my house. If you're an animal lover, you might want to skip it.

"Words in Collision" is obscene. Anyone who works the border will immediately recognize the obscenities in the essay. I assume it will offend a few readers, though I hope the blood and suffering in the book are more upsetting than a cornucopia of bad words.

"A Day in the Life" is my small Norman Mailer project. I consider it a nonfiction novella. It is composed of stories from three different families; one lives in the former dump, one lives in the active dump, and one lived in a strange outland, away from either dump, in a melancholy twilight. I have tried to use novelistic techniques to get at a deeper truth. The story comes from spending thousands of hours in the life, and I thought three extraordinary days of three ordinary families might combine to give you a sense of what it's like to be them.

The rest of the book is self-explanatory.

> This is pure and undefiled religion in the sight of our God and Father, to visit orphans and widows in their distress, and to keep oneself untainted by the world.
> —James 1:27

The Rabin assassination is on all the televisions. They watch it with deep interest in Tijuana. Tijuana itself has been exposed to political violence lately, and the city is still trying to come to grips with it.

They watch the images from the other side of the globe, and I'm told they are amazed at what they see. Not at the footage of Rabin being carried away, nor of the rallies or the mourning. They are amazed at the land.

They press forward and point. Hebron. Golan. They are amazed: the West Bank! Why, it looks exactly like Tijuana.

A Lake
of Sleeping Children

Just when you think you've seen it all, Tijuana comes up with something so unexpected that you may not, at first, be sure what you're seeing. And then, when you do figure it out, likely as not you'll be stunned into silence and have to just stand there, staring. It's happened again: Tijuana threw me a curveball.

Since I am lately seen as some kind of expert on Tijuana's poverty, I often find myself leading mini-safaris to the southland's favorite representation of hell. You know the drill by now: we go to some shacks, maybe stop at an orphanage or two, gobble fish tacos and go to Tacos El Paisano, then gird ourselves for the Tijuana dump. Everybody loves the dump—cameras fly out of purses, and wanderers walk into the trash, furtively glancing at me over their shoulders so they can be sure they're not *really* in danger.

If there aren't a million gulls, some living-dead pit-bull mongrel bitches, or overwhelming stenches rising in eye-watering clouds, the tourists feel cheated and blue. But the sight of an open and festering wound, say, on a garbage-picker's hand . . . well! That sends them right over the moon. Pus Polaroids for the apocalypse scrapbook.

It seems to me that the gringos at the King Kong Group,

those sultans of NAFTA trash operating the dump and si-
phoning easy millions off the efforts of these hungry *basureros*,
could open an amusement park ride right here. Hieronymus
Bosch Land: The Garden of Earthly Delights Ride in 3-D
Stinkovision!

And there I was, leading a small safari yet again. And when
I got to the lake of sleeping children, it took me a while to see
what I was looking at. And of course I'm exaggerating: it
wasn't nearly a lake; it was a pond, a lagoon. And the smell
was as vivid as we'd all hoped. And later, when I tried to sleep,
I knew the thing had seeped into me. It gets into you, you
know—it gets in through the eyes. You find pieces of it drifting in your head as you sleep, and you're infected. I dreamed,
later, of the children. They were waking up. They were sitting up. The filthy water was cascading out of their eye sock-
ets. They opened their mouths to call my name, and black
water jetted out, like fountains.

And, my God, *they wanted to play with me.*

Those of us who worked with the poor all those years in Baja
saw so many astounding things that we could each make a full
album of them. Things at once horrific and sly, with a kind of
Salvador Dalí sense of demonic humor. Droll sights, and almost metaphoric in their richness.

Like the day when I came across the refrigerator in the
Barrio of Shallow Graves (near the blinking TV antennas you
can see from San Diego, ghostly over the middle ground of
Tijuana). I opened the door—it wasn't connected to any
power source, just sitting on the edge of a dirty alley, more
Magritte than Dalí—and sitting on the middle shelf, in the
middle of the middle shelf, on a small tin serving tray, was
one curled, perfectly formed human turd. Presented taste-
fully, as if it were some kind of evil finger sandwich.

Like the woman who swore she was suffering from the evil eye. And when the *curandera* came to cast out the demons, a small viper fell out of the straw seat of the kitchen chair she was sitting on and writhed in the dirt beneath her. "I feel better," the woman said.

Like the man who lived in a washing-machine box. He didn't like sleeping on the dirt, so he carpeted the floor with cast-off avocados. He slept in a blackening swamp of guacamole.

Like the time Negra was given a pair of pigs as a gift. Now, Negra is quite a farmer; she has a knack for growing flowers in the trash, for bringing up various creatures and selling them—dogs, cats, crows, geese, pigs. The pigs in question were those cute little potbellied fellows, about the size of small cats when she first got them. When I first saw them in the corner of her house, I mistook them for puppies. I was startled to pick one up and have it shriek, "Greet! Greeeeet!"

It never occurred to the giver, nor to me, that Negra and all her neighbors had never heard of a mini-pig. In fact, the very concept of a mini-pig was so extraordinary as to be indecipherable to them. When I tried to explain what kind of pigs these were, she looked at me as if I were crazy.

Needless to say, the pigs refused to grow into fat giant porkers. Negra fed and fed them—overfed them, in fact. Gave them vitamins. And then, when it was obvious that an evil curse had been put on these shoats ("They stay babies no matter what we do!" Negra said), she called in the handy witch-doctor, who used up most of her family savings casting spell after spell, trying to break the powerful black hoodoo curse that kept these potential bacon factories chained to infancy.

◻ ◻ ◻ ◻

Tony, a United pilot and book dealer, was in town for his mother's wedding. We had met through the book business and were starting a friendship. Because of the nature of the writing life, you travel about once a month, or more, and end up in all kinds of unlikely places. You're seldom home, or at least I have been seldom home, and a United pilot is a good guy to have for a friend, since he's able to show up in many of the cities you're visiting. It is always good to see a friendly face—or, I should say, a face you know. All the faces are usually friendly: everybody but the Tijuana police, Pat Buchanan, and the Nestor Militia likes an author. (One night I was standing around in the lobby of a hotel in San Francisco, chatting with a bunch of really pleasant British bankers. All of them gray-haired, vaguely weathered, wearing jackets and Oxford shirts and saying "Lovely" and "Quite right." It was only when the elevator doors were closing that I realized I'd been chatting with Pink Floyd.)

And Tony had read about the *dompe* and wanted to see it. I think he may have wanted to compare it with his mental pictures of Saigon. I think his nose was secretly longing for that weird tropical rot you get stuck in there: mangoes and mud and something dead and some sewage mixed in with flowers.

The dump was quiet.

Once a gaping Grand Canyon, it gradually filled with the endless glacier of trash until it rose, rose, swelling like a filling belly. The canyon filled and formed a flat plain, and the plain began to grow in bulldozed ramps, layers, sections, battlements. New American garbology affected the basic Mexican nature of the place. From a disorderly sprawl of *basura* to a kind of Tower of Babel of refuse.

Still, the poor Mexicans, transformed now by NAFTA into a kind of squadron of human tractors, made their way through the dump, lifting, sifting, bagging, hauling, carting, plucking, cutting, recycling. The original *dompe* rules, a set of ordinances that sprang up organically from the people who have to work the garbage, prevailed. A set of rules, by the way, that are extraordinarily humane and sane.

In the midsection of the *dompe*, the big trucks drop off their loads, and the towering orange tractors, roaring and farting and crushing the mounds with nasty steel wheels sporting *Mad Max* knobs and spikes, pass by with the seeming arrogance of a *T. rex* hunting party.

There, of course, the best stuff is to be found. The strong and the young work this dangerous zone. Anything is possible here. The freshest produce, the undented cans, the unbroken televisions, the bursting bags, the brightest stenches, the runniest of the rotted wads of refuse, the startling explosions of dead dogs, cats, horses, jump out of the tumbling comic books and soda cans and soggy Pampers like some strange carnal jack-in-the-box.

You sometimes have to drop down into the trash. There are gaps in the piles. And if you get down into the gap, into the *basura* fault line, you have a side view of strata. You might find a six-pack of Dole pineapple juice lodged in there like trilobites. It's part mining, part farming, part archaeology. (Some visitors to Negra's house declined water on a hot day, so she graciously broke out some cool cans of orange juice. "Don't tell them," she said, "I got those out of the trash with a shovel.")

When you do drop down in there, you put up a pole with a rag tied at the end. This alerts the tractor-pilots, who would never see you otherwise, to veer away from your hole and spare your life.

Rule #1: Watch for heavy machinery. Those who do not become mulch.

Rule #2: No children in the trash.

Rule #3: Women are equal to men in the trash.

Rule #4: Old-timers and kids are allowed to work the outer edges of the trash, where the tractors push things down the slopes and the slopes themselves act as sifters, rolling the best things out across the face of the new King Kong pyramid.

Rule #5: A special safe area is set up by the healthy workers. This area is set apart, avoided by the trucks and the tractors. It has inviolate boundaries, could almost be roped off. And everybody honors it. The occasional truckload is directed over there, or young men carry a few bags there and toss them in. In this special section, the disabled and the old are allowed to do their share. They can work all day, safely, aside, not competed with or jostled or in harm's way. But working hard, nonetheless.

There is no welfare in the dump, but there is work, care, sweat, and dignity.

The dump could be described as a series of arcs.

There is the small arc of a hill that hides the dump from view. This hill sits between the dump and the view of San Diego. Running along the other side of this hill is a curving road that leads down to barrios at one end and Tijuana at the other.

Behind this hill, the next arc: the narrow village that has sprung up. These homes are where the majority of the modern garbage-pickers dwell. And Tony pointed out that it seemed a pretty well-off community. Certainly better off than Vietnam had been. *(Yeah, no napalm—yet.)* After all, there are chickens and dogs, kites rattling in the power lines; there are power lines!

The next arc: the potter's field. At the top of a rise the

crematorium, and in the middle distance the adult graves, and then at the lower end the babies. The graves with cribs for headstones, where parents bring their small daughters and sons and scratch out their final beds in the yellow dirt. *Niña, 3 días*, the crooked wooden crosses say. Or *María de los Angeles, Julio 3–Julio 5*. Or *Hijo. Un día*. Or the cribs, forlorn and somehow frightening, still vaguely cheery in their colors as they come apart in the elements, fade, break, slump. Playpens. And a board hammered onto the side that bears the sad, minuscule life history of yet another *niña* or *niño*.

Then the final arc, a sort of bull's-eye: the dump.

We walked along, looking, and then we saw the lake and stopped and it started to lap at the edges of our minds, the dark water, the realization of what it was we were seeing, the strange shore of a land so far from home, so far from Tijuana even, that we could have been glimpsing the lip of the underworld. We could have been wading in the feces-scented waters of the River Styx.

Miraculously peculiar things abound in the dump, too. If you have an eye for the perversely beautiful, you can have a wonderful day looking around. I have seen tornados of garbage rising thirty feet in the air. I have seen piles of money tumbling in the landslide of shattering windows and dancing shoes. Three-legged dogs? All the time. Try a two-legged dog, running at full speed balanced on his two legs and zooming into the distance like a living rollerblade.

One day I thought I was seeing little geysers or volcanoes. But Negra pointed out that a subterranean trash fire had started. But it hadn't remained in the trash: it had crept into the graves. And the dry carcasses of these dear people were igniting underground. Sometimes, when it rained, the ground actually broke open and flames leapt up for a moment.

This day, somehow, there had been a flood.

Tony the pilot first saw it. One end of the dump had been closed off by the new trash mountain. A small valley had been sealed at one end, where the runoff would have originally formed a nostalgic little waterfall into the little Edward Abbey desert canyon and run on to the sea. Deer would have frolicked at its base; jackrabbits, coyotes, foxes, hawks, owls, rattlesnakes, tarantulas, three kinds of daisies, locoweed, gourds, raccoons, lizards, tortoises, skunks, wild goats, cottonwoods, berries, grapes, small fish, crawdads, butterflies, pottery shards, arrowheads, lions, morning glories, corn, Queen Anne's lace, would have flourished along this glittering little creek. Now, however, the northern arm of the landfill had cut off the vale and the small bed of the waterway. The canyon itself, as we know, was long gone. Kotex, Keds, Kalimán comic books, and ketchup bottles frolicked there now.

The slopes of this vale, small as it was, were crowded with the sad wooden crosses of the dead children's graves. The whole area was full of nameless, abandoned, forgotten, sleeping little corpses. Plastic flowers faded from blue to pink by the sun. A toy or two. Cribs.

From somewhere this flood had come. And the vale filled with water. And the water ate away at the slope, the clay and sand coming loose and the little crosses toppling and falling into the water to float around like model sailboats. And other crosses, those in the bottom of the vale, stood in the water at angles, reflecting on the still surface. It looked like a Pink Floyd album cover, actually.

And all around the edge of this lake (I always think of it as a *lake*, not a pond, a pool) was stinking mud, and stuck to the mud at every angle were more crosses. Broken crosses. Crooked crosses. Scattered crosses. Fallen crosses. Names on some, peering up at me from the lapping water's edge: Juan, Hija, Nena, Linda.

At one side, three vast tractor tires. They marched into the water in a row. The one farthest out we couldn't see into. The middle one was empty, save for some dark water and some blown trash. The one on the shore had become an impromptu outhouse: it was well loaded, the shit falling on crosses. Shit on the painstakingly handpainted letters: *Diciembre 21–Dic. 25; Mi Hijo; Alfonsina, 10 días y 4 horas.*

And crowding the shore, gulls. Many, many gulls. Gulls fighting, pushing, raising their wings but not flying. Fat and noisy gulls. We stood there watching them, this white snowdrift of gulls. And they'd waddle to the water and heave themselves into it. Filthy water. Black at first, but with a clear blue overlay of sky. Floating with wads of paper and bits of wood and these gulls and the reflections and shadows of the crosses standing out there like mangroves in a swamp.

And the gulls dipped their heads into the water and brought up small tidbits and flung their heads back and gulped.

And the water revealed small brown and green and reddish objects. A kind of layer beneath the surface, like seaweed. Like the clouds of stuff in miso soup. Like algae, but not algae. And we looked: looked at the shore, where the ground was swelling with this noxious water and crumbling. And we looked in, deep, where the bed of the lake was mud, and the mud was drifting up, and the rotten soil was broken, and the coffins, the cardboard boxes, the pillowcases, the wooden crates, the winding sheets, were coming up. They were coming up. The children themselves were rising, expanding into the water, and the gulls were eating them.

The gulls had grown too fat to fly on the flesh of these sleeping children.

The sky above was yet another perfect southern California blue. The blue of a stained glass window. Clouds as bright as electric signs over our heads. And that same sky, spreading farther than any of us can know, shading different colors in different places, covered the garbage dump in Mexico City, the garbage dump in Manila, the garbage dumps in El Salvador, Guatemala, Zaire, Rwanda, Honduras, Mexicali, Matamoros, Juárez, Belize, Ho Chi Minh City, Patpong, Calcutta, Sarajevo, Tripoli, New Jersey, and Three Mile Island, Pennsylvania.

Proposition 187? A new Berlin Wall at the border? California citizen identification cards? Microchips injected into the backs of our hands, read by circling Landsat spy satellites? Two thousand Border Patrol guards augmented by T-1000 Terminator Droids armed with nuclear shotguns and laser-sighting eyeballs?

You think they're going to work? You think they can possibly work? Swim in this lake for a minute, then tell me you can keep these people on its shore. Jump in—you own it: it's Lake Nafta.

Dompe Days

One: The Infinite Swirl

Imagine this: a muscular storm came in during the last days, and as we drove into the Tijuana dump, we were greeted by an apocalyptic scene. Let me try to describe it. The dump, as you know, is cheek by jowl with a rangy home-built cemetery. In fact, many of the graves are partially covered by trash. The garbage used to be in a canyon about 150 feet deep; it is now a hill about 40 feet high. Above this hill is a seething crown of 10,000 gulls, crows, pigeons. But mostly gulls. Imagine, further, mud. Running yellow mud; brown, reddish, black wastewater mixed with dust, ashes, and clay. The few graves with cement slabs over them glisten with the rain. The mud is a gray so dark it verges on black. The sky is raging. Knots of clouds speed east, far above the gulls, and the gulls rise so high that they seem an optical illusion: from huge birds to nearly invisible specks in the sky, they seem to hang on wires, a mad museum display, held in place by the violent wind.

Now we drive in, and the muddy graves are pale blue and pale green and pale brown as their wooden crosses fade; the cement headstones are all white or streaked rainy gray. And from the hill of trash, hundreds, perhaps thousands, of plastic bags—tan bags, blue bags, white supermarket bags, black trash bags, yellow bread wrappers and video store bags—along with long streamers of computer paper, sheets of notebook paper, newspapers open like wings, ribbons of toilet paper, tissues like dancing moths, even half-dead balloons, are caught in a backdraft and are rising and falling in vast slow waves behind the hill, slow motion, a ballet in the air of this parti-colored landscape, looking like special effects, like some art department's million-dollar creation, Lucifer's lava lamp, silent, ghostly, stately, for half a mile, turning in the air, rolling, looping.

And up top, exposed to the elements, the garbage is flying like a snowstorm. We lean into it at angles, held up by the wind. The garbage-pickers are wrapped in bags to keep the rain off them. Huge tractors, two stories tall, churn through the mud. And the goo squishes up to our ankles. Boxes, panties, magazines, more bags, always plastic bags, flying and bouncing and shooting off the summit to snow down on the distant village. I watch paper drift down onto the roofs; advertisements for stoves and dog food form sentimental snowdrifts on the housetops.

Beneath us, the slowly revolving magic bags. Above us, the infinite swirl of gulls. And garbage hurricanes lift off all around us: the photographer thirty yards away from the young woman and me is dwarfed by a whirlwind of trash—it rises twenty, thirty feet above his head, and he stands at the apex, shooting us with our arms around each other, holding on in the wind. Her breasts are wet and running with milk. She tells me it tastes sweet and makes her want to vomit. Our eyes run tears from the wind. A pack of dogs tries to attack us, and a mad Indian woman breaks off from signaling passing Aeromexico jets, hoping they'll land in the *dompe* and take her on a trip. Her name is Doña Chuy. "They'll kill you!" she yells. "The dogs! They'll kill you!" She wades into the pack and knocks them aside with her knees. They snap at her skirt. "Out of my way," she says. "Can't you see a plane is coming in?"

She thinks anti-union death squads are after her.

"I am a revolutionary," she says.

The young woman swirls her finger beside her temple.

"*Está loca*," she says.

"They held a machine gun to my head," says Chuyita.

One scraggly bitch breaks away from the dog pack and runs at me. She has long dark teats that swing beneath her belly, and one eye is ripped out of its socket, and pus and blood are caked to her face, and she makes me want to vomit and run but throws herself at my legs and reveals herself to be the world's sweetest dog, and she rubs herself on me and wags and grins and begs to be petted. So I try to find a spot free of pus.

Behind us, as the rain begins again, a funeral procession wends its way down the narrow mud tracks. Men in wet cowboy hats and boots pull shovels out of a station wagon and wrestle a coffin over the hillocks to a likely spot; ladies with lace veils are buffeted by the wind; endless plastic bags blow between them like fleeing ghosts.

And later, in the warmth of her shack, the young woman I have known since she was six nurses her daughter, and we smile as the little mouth gobbles the huge black nipple, both the mother and I aware that she has chosen today to allow me to see her bare breasts, and we hold hands as the rain hammers at the tar paper.

Can you imagine such a scene?

Two: Boys' Life

Nobody knew what happened to the boys' parents. Not even the boys—Chacho, Eduardo, Jorge, and Carlos (fake names)—could explain what had happened to them. As is so often the case on the border, one day the boys woke up and their parents were gone. Papá had apparently gone across the wire, into the United States. Mamá blew away like a puff of smoke. The four brothers were alone in the Tijuana garbage dump.

For a few nights the younger boys wept as Chacho, the fierce elder brother, pulled together a small homestead amid the garbage. They went hungry for a while, not having any dump survival skills. The trash-pickers gave them what food they could spare, but that wasn't much. And missionaries came to the dump with goodies, but Chacho didn't trust gringos, so he kept the boys away. Besides, the gringos gave baths, and nobody was going to get Chacho naked.

One day an old man appeared in the dump. He wore grimy old suits and had no past and no home. His left arm had come out of the socket years before, and he had wandered, half crippled, from dump to dump, looking for people to care for him. Although there is no lack of ferocity in the *dompes*, there is also a high degree of compassion and fraternity. Still, if you have no food or room to spare, what can you do? Slip him a gringo doughnut *(una dona)* and see him off with a blessing. The evil ones, circling through the waters of night, kicked him around for fun, stole the *dona*, and left him in the dirt.

Chacho came across him after one such beating. He made the old man a deal: if he would look out for the younger boys,

Chacho and Eduardo would share their trash-pickings with him. And Chacho would beat up anyone who threatened the old man. They engineered a new family unit that day.

The old man, keeping his part of the bargain, scrounged a cast-off Maytag appliance box. He cut a door in its side and upended it, open top to the ground. Then he carpeted the dirt floor with newspaper, plastic bags, and cardboard. They used scavenged clothes and rags for a mattress and blankets. The little ones played in the dirt outside while the old man lay in the dark box crying, hallucinating and seeing visions—dead women he had loved, angels, demons, strange creatures, his mother coming to feed him, gringos with bags of beans, which turned out to be us, though I was never sure if he knew he wasn't dreaming.

He had a passion for avocados, and he collected them in rotting mounds inside the box.

For his part, Chacho built a real shack out of scrap wood, and he placed it on a low rise near the Maytag house, where he could watch over his brothers. For whatever reason, it never occurred to him to build them a house—that was the old man's job. Somehow Chacho acquired a pistol. Then he stole a pony from a neighboring ranch and built it a corral made of bedsprings and stolen wood. Chacho was a small warlord, surveying his kingdom.

His brothers watched the clean kids coming out of the gringo baths. They didn't envy the washed faces or clean clothes. They envied the doughnuts and chocolate milk and bananas. They marched into the bathing room and took off their blackened clothes.

Eduardo brought home animals—unwanted puppies, piglets swiped or bartered, a pathetic skeletal cat.

Chacho used his pony to steal cows.

□ □ □ □

Nobody knows what happened to the old man. He was such a phantom that he passed through this story without a name. Perhaps he grew tired of being a dad, of living on a floor of smashed avocados and mud. Or he simply forgot them as the rising tide of mania and tequila ate his brain. Or he was taken by a car in the gloom of the highway canyons. Maybe he tried to go across the border. Any guess, any guess at all, is valid. The boys were out working the trash, and when they came home, he was gone. He had taken their ball of twine, so they knew he had tied his arm to his side. This suggested to them that he was planning a substantial journey.

Like abandoned children everywhere, they felt fear and talked themselves into feeling hope. *He'll be back. Maybe he'll bring us some food.* They huddled around the door of the box all night. When morning came, they knew they were alone again.

They marched up to Chacho's bandit's roost to seek help, to move in with him at least. But Chacho was a busy man. He was a *pistolero* and a cattle rustler, and he was suspected of being an undercover snitch for the police. He had *socios* (what we would call homeboys) running errands and fencing goods for him. He had a television. And he had his pistol.

Look, boys, he told them, the point is that life's shit. Who coddled me? Nobody. Who felt sorry for me? You see this house? These horses? This *pistola?* I did this. You've got to go out there and make your lives. Be tough or die.

This, in Chacho's eyes, was love.

Eduardo, Jorge, and Carlos failed to be moved by Chacho's warm sentiments. But they had to obey. He was, after all, their big brother. The closest thing to an elder they had. He was also macho, and they were afraid that if they whined too much, he'd pull his six-shooter and do them in. He wore it jammed in his belt, and even wore it to intimidate the missionaries. I once heard him say, near Pastor Von's van, "I'd better like these doughnuts. I'd hate to shoot anybody." This statement, as all macho bon mots, was delivered with a scowl that hid a tremendous laughter. Pancho Villa is the patron saint of machismo, and Pancho Villa is the in-dwelling spirit of every macho. Anyone who has survived in a tough area knows: machos are philosophers, and they are also weary judges of all they survey. If their variable code of ethics is betrayed, they are often called upon by their inner demons to be executioners. *A man's gotta do what a man's gotta do.* A macho can explode in unreasoning fury or act with benign munificence, at a moment's notice. Machos are sentimentalists, like all true fascists. Robin Hood or Vlad the Impaler—whichever it is, you have to have what it takes to back up the pose.

Chacho didn't like it, but he sent them away. That is not to say that Chacho lost any sleep over his brothers. Not yet.

Boys living on the edges of the dump have a vast playground of sorts. Collecting trash is hard work, even if the trash-picking is off to the side, where the small ones can go. The brothers played and romped in the mounds, found the occasional toy, found clothes and tins of food, found waterlogged magazines with pictures of nude women, which they took to Chacho. Once they even found a load of fetuses dumped on the edge of the trash. "Dead babies," everyone was saying. "A sacrifice." People were afraid, able to envision only something desperately evil, something monumental that would kill so many babies, then toss them into the dump. The boys poked at the cold fetuses with sticks. To them, living in such squalor, something even more squalid was a revelation.

Although Eduardo loved animals, for example, the sight of

a diseased dog being pounced upon and eaten by other dogs was exciting.

The boys had rats to kill, fires to set, food to steal, huts to spy on. No wall in that neighborhood was particularly solid, and they could peek in through the cracks and see just about anything. And there were always the fights to watch: drunks and gang members and warring young turks from alien barrios and young women throwing punches like the meanest macho. Small Huck Finns on a sea of trash, they floated through life, avoiding schooling and being educated by the harsh classroom all around them.

They even had their own swimming hole.

On the hill above Chacho's horse pens, the city had built a huge *pila* to hold water for the downhill communities. The part of the reservoir above ground was the size of a *maquiladora* or a warehouse, and it didn't take long for the boys to break through an upper corner of the cinderblock structure. They climbed in through the hole with their pals and sat on the walkways in the shadows within. They loved to swim in that cool green water. They loved to urinate in the water, imagining their pee going down the hill to the fine stucco homes.

The one game they loved the most was the most dangerous. Everyone, even Chacho, warned them about it. Everyone told them to stop. But they loved it to the point of madness. The boys loved to jump on the backs of moving garbage trucks.

Eduardo thought he had a firm grip on the back of the big truck.

Retired from San Diego, the truck was rusty and dented. It was heavy with trash, and greasy fluids drained out of its sides

like sweat. Its hunched back was dark with dirt, and its smoke-
stack belched solid black clouds.

The boys had spent the morning running up behind the
trucks as they entered the dump, hopping on the back ends,
hanging on to any handhold they could grab. Sometimes, if
they missed, they caught the sides and hung there like little
spiders, swinging over the wheelwells as the trucks banged
over the mounds.

Eduardo had run behind the truck, had flung himself at it
and caught the upper edge of the open maw in back. He
swung back and forth, doing an impromptu trapeze act, and
the other boys called insults: "Faggot!" and "Coward!" He
turned once to laugh at them, hanging by one hand and starting to flash them a hand sign. The truck slammed on its
brakes. Eduardo flew inside, hit the steel wall, and was flung
back out, hitting the ground on his back, hard enough to
knock the breath out of him.

The boys were laughing wildly, and Eduardo tried to rise,
pasting a game smile on his face though the blow must have
hurt. He probably couldn't catch his breath. He lay back, just
for an instant, to breathe.

The truck ground its gears and lurched into reverse. The
boys yelled for Eduardo to get out of the way, but it must
have sounded like more taunting. He raised one hand. The
truck backed over him and the hand was twisted down to the
ground, and the double wheels in the back made Eduardo
disappear.

Carlos and Jorge stood staring, imagining somehow that
Eduardo would get up after the truck had passed over him.
But he was deep in the soil, in a puddle of his own mud. The
truck driver shut off the engine and stepped out to unload the
garbage, but he couldn't understand why the boys were
screaming.

Three: Boot Hill

The dump people don't always knit together. Sheer survival makes it difficult to look out for their fellows. But death sometimes unites them, if the death is sad enough. Or the threat of death, if the threat is vivid enough.

Everyone knew Eduardo's story. They had all said at one time or another that someone should do something about those boys, but nobody had done much. They had all seen the Maytag box, the old man, the truck-surfing. Guilty and ashamed, the neighbors resolved to do something about Eduardo's death.

They collected money. Centavos came from hidden beer money, from the jar under the bed, from the schoolbook fund, from Christmas savings. The *americanos* gave funds. People worked extra hard that day to get a few more pesos.

They bought Eduardo a small suit. His first and last fancy clothes. Some of the Mixtec men collected raw particleboard and hammered together a coffin. They set it inside the room where the missionaries gave baths. This was done very quickly. No undertaker ever saw Eduardo, no papers were ever signed. No official ever knew he had existed, and none would be told he had died.

Since he wasn't embalmed, they had to hurry. The suit was bought and pulled onto his twisted corpse by nightfall. The coffin was built by eight P.M., and he was laid out under candles by nine. The women had washed his face. Eduardo was finally clean.

They would bury him in the morning.

□ □ □ □

Chacho took a bath. He stuck his pistol into his belt, got drunk, and walked over to weep over Eduardo. All the tough guys in the dump lost it over Eduardo. None of them knew how to deal with this tragedy. It was somehow worse than all the other tragedies. The men wept openly, inconsolably. Perhaps Eduardo had come to symbolize their own abandonment. Perhaps this small boy, thrown into the trash, left to die there, and facing a burial there, was too much like all of them. There was no way they were going to bury him in the trash too. In being killed, Eduardo had become everybody's son, everybody's brother. One family boasted that they had fed him often, another bragged that he wore their old shoes. Girls wrote his name on little torn bits of paper—hearts and flowers in blue Bic ink. Every boy there claimed Eduardo as his best friend. You would think somebody had actually loved him.

Chacho got one of his *socios* to drive a pickup. They hammered the lid on the box, then wrestled it up on their shoulders. The people who had not gone to work—mostly wives and daughters—stood silently. A woman or two worked her rosary beads. Some cried—nothing overwhelming, but there were tears. The boys lifted the box over the side and placed it carefully in the bed. Chacho and his remaining brothers climbed in with Eduardo.

Directly behind the pickup was a flatbed. It was filled to capacity with mourners. They passed a bottle of rum. Chacho would be drinking plenty that night and the next. People would steer clear of his robber's cabin, because Chacho would be in the mood to shoot.

Bringing up the rear of this funeral procession was one gringo van with a few missionaries. That one detail has lived on in the neighborhood, that the *americanos* came to bury Eduardo. Nobody asked them. They just appeared. Mourning. It was the most anyone had ever done for the people on the hill.

Ironically, a busload of fresh-faced American Jesus Teens from some suburban church had pulled up and unloaded thirty happy campers into the middle of the funeral. They bounded about Praising the Lord and Ministering to the Poor. They were no doubt shocked to find the poor rather surly and unappreciative of their Witness. Their youth pastor, being no slouch, took the opportunity to send them into the shed before Eduardo was sealed into his box. He wanted the kids to learn what real life was like. For his part, Eduardo gave them a devastating sermon, lying there in his already dusty suit, flat and angry-looking. A mute testimony.

All the bounce gone out of their strides, the teens mounted their bus again and motored away, easy answers scrubbed right out of their skulls.

During all this, Carlos, the youngest of the brothers, stayed outside, playing marbles. He didn't show the least interest in Eduardo's corpse. As Chacho was standing beside the coffin, crying out his pain, Carlos used him as a sort of shield, peering around him at Eduardo. He reached out and prodded Eduardo's face with his fingers, apparently to make sure his brother was really dead. He then went outside and joined the marble game.

They could have been going to work, hauling some junk to the dump.

The small procession headed off across the hills, winding through small valleys and into regions never visited by gringos. They left the road entirely and drove across dead fields. Up a hill. Some of the dump people had created their own graveyard there. Little crosses made of sticks dotted the hill.

The dead here were squatters. One day the landowner would find out. But really, how can you fight with the dead?

One American said, "It's Boot Hill."

The men traded turns with the shovel, cracking, then scraping out the rocky soil. It took quite a while to make the hole, but between them, they managed it. Nobody complained.

They manhandled the box into the hole and stood around looking at it. Chacho almost fell in, he cried so hard. The men quietly went back to work, pushing dirt and rocks back in. Others who couldn't get close to the shoveling went from grave to grave, pulling dry weeds and picking up paper. Some of the crosses needed straightening. A couple of guys made borders of rocks around unmarked graves.

Jorge never went near Eduardo's grave.

But if you paid close attention, you could see Carlos moving in behind Chacho. He peeked out from between Chacho's legs. Then, at the last possible moment, he grabbed a little handful of dust and pitched it into the hole.

The Pink Penitentiary

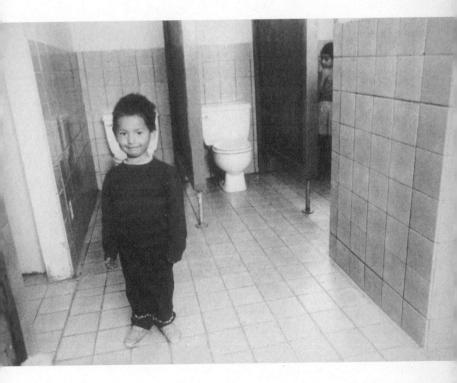

We will call the orphanage el Jardín de Rosas.

Six A.M. The dogs have been awake for an hour already, charging back and forth between the gates, growling at passing trucks and the drunks lurching home from all-night parties. In the compound, the chickens are clucking, and the voices of the boys can be heard. A cement basketball court lies upon the dirt of the big yard. On it, one small boy lies facedown, asleep. His partner, who is ten years old, is still up. He's swaying with exhaustion, but he's still awake because he knows if he's found asleep, he'll have to kneel out here all night again. The boys get in trouble. He stole gum; his sleeping buddy got in a fistfight. When these things happen, the orphanage director, who lives high above them in his apartment perched atop the building, comes down, scolds them, makes them read Bible verses, then forces them to kneel on the cement. All night. It happens to everybody, sooner or later.

Rubén, the oldest boy, is now in the kitchen, opening cans and cracking eggs. Rubén is worried—two of the other older boys have been sodomizing each other when they think the other boys in the dormitory are asleep. But Rubén is up later than everyone else. He wants to be a missionary to the Tarahumara Indians of Chihuahua, the famous and mysterious tribe of runners, who regularly engage in hundred-mile races wearing leather huaraches on their feet. He studies his Bible late into the night, and after lights out, he thinks about the scriptures.

He turns to the book of Hebrews, *Hebreos, capítulo trece, versículos dos y tres:* "Do not neglect to show hospitality to strangers, for by this some have entertained angels without knowing it. Remember the prisoners, as though in prison with them, and those who are ill-treated, since you yourselves are also in the body."

Lying there, he hears the boys whisper, then the blanket on each bed rustle, and the sly creak of the springs. One of the boys has been reprimanded before for coercing littler boys to have oral sex with him. Rubén doesn't know what to do. He doesn't want to be a squealer, but he knows what they're doing is a sin. And it upsets him greatly to listen to the rhythmic creaking of the bed frame.

In the kitchen, he hauls out the huge frying pans. The cook, a young woman who lives at the far end of the compound with her husband, is the only female in the orphanage, save for the director's wife and daughter. And Hermana Conchita, a strange crone who lives in a small storage room beside the big room where they keep the clothes and shoes and blankets.

The cook rifles through the hundred loaves of old bread donated by the gringos, trying to find enough slices that are not moldy. If they're stiff and dried out, she toasts them. The boys won't notice. The bad slices can go to the dogs and the chickens. She melts lard and Rubén begins cracking more than a hundred eggs. This morning there will be forty-two boys at the table, along with a couple of adults.

Some of the younger boys who worship Rubén make pests of themselves as they scurry around behind him, trying to help.

Ezekiel is almost blind. He's sleeping in the nursery this week, keeping watch on the little ones. He changes their diapers and hustles them to the dual toilets raised on a pedestal to the rear of the room. There, pairs of little boys grunt away while the others watch. Ezekiel's thick glasses make him seem humorous; his eyes through the lenses are huge and seem to float beyond the plane of his face. Like a cartoon. And he jokes with them, able to be hip among the two-year-olds: "*Orale, morros—hagan caca, pues.*" (All right, little dudes, make that poo!) His brother is addicted to glue and has melted enough of his brain so that he seems to slosh somehow, his ideas loose in his head and runny.

Upstairs, the boys are stirring. Their bunk beds smell of urine. The boys are grumpy, dressed in their street clothes because they don't have enough blankets. Well, they have enough, but the director will not allow them to use them. He's saving them for future use. The one boy who gets two blankets has a bunk up against a shattered window. He sleeps year-round in the blowing air. When it rains hard, he sometimes tucks some cardboard in the hole to keep the water off him. The director applauds this. He likes to see such initiative. But he doesn't fix the window.

Radios are a sin, unless they're tuned to a Christian station. However, the Christian stations are sinful because they play music with drums. Drums in all their forms are evil: they convey the Satanic beats of Negro religion. All drums are instruments of voodoo and pagan cult activity. Hence, the so-called Jesus rock is a deception that is misleading the Saints in these Last Days. Likewise electrically amplified instruments. Electric guitars are evil both in sound and intent, though country-western and *ranchera* music utilize them, so the director is sometimes willing to make exceptions.

Rock and roll, as always, is more powerful than authority. It's everywhere. He's exhausted from trying to catch every demonic sex-inducing radio. Often he just walks by the boys as they listen to the Devil's Music and shakes his head. They know what he thinks—maybe this Witness is enough. Later in life, perhaps his example will pull them away from some evil deed. He tells himself that the very fact that he's tired and can't keep up with rock music is proof of how evil it is.

Downstairs, there is a great commotion. Hermana Conchita is beating one of the boys.

Most of the older boys hate her. Many of them have never known a mother, or have only seen her on three or four weekends a year. Hermana Conchita is about it.

She uses a rubber hose. When she flies into one of her unexplained rages, she flogs the boys around the shoulders and faces with it, beating them into corners where they can't escape. The director, in his fourth-floor aerie, says it's not true.

She's got the hose now, and she's swinging.

Hermana Conchita has a problem, though. She didn't count of growing old—or on her charges getting bigger. It's the law of diminishing returns. Many of her victims tower over her now, and they could easily break her arm. As she pounds one of the little boys, he's heartened by the jeers of the bigger boys, whom she cannot hurt now. Her hose whacks the little guy across the shoulders, and he winces, then he starts to laugh at her.

"Witch," Ezekiel taunts. "Hag. Bitch" (*perra:* female dog,

not evil woman). "Hit me now," he says, his headlamp eyes bright behind the lenses. "Hit me now." He's hopping around on one foot, hands held up as if to box. Ezekiel is as cool as they get this morning. The other boys call him Cheque (*Chéh-keh*), and they call this nickname out to him, urging him on.

Everybody's scuffling around in a loose knot, flowing up and down the big yard. The kneeling boy has yet to be released from his sentence. His buddy has awakened and blessed his good luck and struggled back up on his knees, undiscovered. To protect himself, though, he has had to throw bloody warnings all about him: "You tell him I fell asleep, and *you'll get yours!*" he threatens. What they don't know is that the director is watching gringo television and eating donated waffles upstairs; he has forgotten all about them and won't remember till he sees them when he wanders down. They watch the Conchita-baiting with dull fascination.

"What are we doing in school today?" one asks the other.

But the boy doesn't answer. He has started to cry.

"Aw, come on," his buddy says.

"I want my mother," the boy says.

"Well," the first boy says, "she'll probably come this weekend. You'll see."

"Really?" he says. And he wipes his nose on his sleeve.

The toilets are full to the brim. They are brown and solid, and of the four, two are running over. A thin slick of shit seeps across the floor and makes a scum at the drain hole. The boys sometimes put their feet on the rim and let fly from a foot high. There is a sign written on the plywood partitions between the toilets. Someone has written it with charcoal. Maybe Rubén—he's thoughtful enough to have done it.

The sign says:

PLEASE DON'T SHIT ON THE FLOOR
PLEASE DON'T WIPE YOUR ASS WITH YOUR
  FINGERS
PLEASE DON'T WIPE YOUR FINGERS ON THE
  WALL

Ancient brown fingerprints and smears angle away from this notice, trailing to faint shadow. They look like paintings of comets, of fireworks.

Fausto has a chicken. This chicken rides on his shoulders. His father brought him in and said, "He's no good. I want nothing to do with him." Fausto kept a stony face the whole time. "You can have him," his father said. "I don't care what you do with him."

Once Fausto ran away to try to find his mother. He traveled deep into Mexico, knowing she was some sort of cantina girl. He was about thirteen, probably. Tall and skinny, with huge eyes that watered easily. He searched in whorehouses in the interior, sleeping under cars, in parks. He finally found his own hometown. When he found the cantina, they told him she had died the week before he got there.

Now he keeps to the chickens. Sometimes he beats up smaller boys. This morning he ignores the fight with Conchita. He hunches down in the small chicken coop the other boys have helped him build. He makes small kisses with his lips. The chicken steps on his wrist, then begins to work its way up to his shoulder, wings held open like the arms of a tightrope walker.

▫ ▫ ▫ ▫

Rubén comes out and claps his hands.

"¡*A comer!*" he orders. (To eat!)

Ezekiel is a little wild with the fight—his face is flushed and he's skipping around, cussing. His brother, still fried from last night's glue-sniffing, eggs him on. Rubén has to grab him and bang some *cocos* (noogies) into the top of his head.

Cheque goes in to eat, rubbing his head and wincing, making deadly threats all around. The boys kneeling ask, "Can we come in?"

Rubén glances up at the director's apartment.

"No," he says.

When they complain, he says, "Next time you'll behave better. Talk to the Lord."

At the huge tables, the boys cram in, elbow to elbow. The director descends. They can hear him asking the boys outside if they're sorry for what they did.

"Yes, sir," they say.

Will they commit such sins again?

"No, sir."

Well, maybe he'll let them up . . . after breakfast. They can clean the kitchen.

They moan.

He comes in.

"Good morning," he says.

"Good morning," they all respond.

"How are we this morning?"

"Fine."

Somebody blurts, "Cheque got in a fight with Conchita."

Cheque's out of his seat. "Liar!" he shouts. "She was using the hose!"

"Cheque," the director warns. "What happens to troublemakers?"

Cheque sits back down, grumbling.

"We'll talk later."

Bold now to save face, Ezekiel murmurs the boys' version of "I don't give a fuck" *(Me vale madre)*.

The director rushes toward him, a small burst of rage in his eyes that makes Cheque flinch. The director's son, somewhat of a hero to the boys, comes in.

"I'll handle it," he tells his father. He goes to Cheque and grabs his shoulder and says, "Let's go outside."

They exit.

"Oh," the boys say.

The director beams. He enjoys happy high jinks. Boys will be boys.

"Let us pray," he says.

It's time for clothes distribution. Before school, the boys petition the orphanage director for shoes, or coats, or pants, or blankets. He stands in the doorway and inspects them.

"My shirt's torn," says one. "I need a new one."

"It's not *my* fault," the director says. "I didn't tear it, did I?"

"But it's torn!"

"You should have thought about that before you tore it!"

"I'll throw this one away!" the boy threatens.

"If you're that stupid," the director quips, "go right ahead!" He laughs. The boys laugh.

"Can I have a new shirt?"

"No."

The buildings are pink. The color of Pepto-Bismol. Neighborhood tough guys are driven to murder by the color. They call orphanage boys "faggots" and "girls."

Fistfights are common.

A small Tijuana park sits about a half-mile from the orphanage. The boys can see it from the big yard. They don't often go there, though, because the *cholos* will beat them up if they catch them on their turf. J, who is a legend in the orphanage because he's having a romance with one of the crazy gringa missionary women who comes every week, has just gotten a sound beating at the hands of the tough guys.

He has a juicy-looking shiner. The gringa almost loses it when she sees his face. She's twice as tall as he and is probably ten years his senior. She will begin making solo trips on Tijuana buses to visit him, bringing him radios, sweaters, candy. When she's gone, J will not answer questions about her directly, but his smile says *breasts, bare bottoms*.

The message of his smile fuels late-night masturbation in the bunks. They all want women. They all want *American* women. He knows it, and it gives him great power.

"Someday," he promises. "Someday, I'll tell you."

In her dark room, Hermana Conchita falls asleep fingering a huge Bible.

They rush off to school.

The dogs take over the big yard. One of the bigger boys thinks it's funny to sneak in to the coop and kill Fausto's chicken. Fausto won't know until this evening, when he comes home in his tired uniform.

The cook stays in the nursery, playing with the little ones. They are a wild gaggle of tykes, and they sometimes descend on her as one, all of them wanting hugs at once. The two boys on the slab are allowed up. The one who fell asleep can walk; the other cannot. The director allows him to stay home from school today. He hobbles off to bed, the director telling him he's a good boy after all. The boy limps past Rubén upstairs. Rubén is packing his things for a stay in San Diego, visiting a gringo church. Rubén knows the others envy him what he's about to receive: hot baths, color TV, ice cream. A big bed, a stereo, clothes, cold soda. Girls. But Rubén is not that interested in physical luxuries. He longs to be an ascetic, a true servant of the Lord. He will trust in God for his daily bread, though he will admit that the thought of a big steak excites him just a little.

Everyone in the orphanage has begun to look upon him differently. Rubén has started to glow.

Cheque has put a T-shirt on under his uniform. It says "Dr. Zogg's Sex Wax." Cheque knows he's cool. He has a small radio and he plays it full blast as he bebops down the dirt road, speaker distorting the Devil's Music into an indecipherable gargle. He shouts out the lyrics and tells the little guys he'll kick everybody's ass if they don't do exactly what he says.

His brother vanishes halfway to school. They'll find him asleep after school. He'll be smiling.

When they get home, the meal cycle will begin again. Then basketball until it's too dark to see. Then bed.

None of them talk about their dreams.

Words in Collision

A curious thing happens in Mexico, especially on the border. The scenario baffles American onlookers, but the Mexicans are beginning to understand.

Here's what happens: a gringo is caught in traffic, say. He's in a good mood. His car's chock-full of plaster bootleg life-size Bart Simpson banks—though in Tijuana he's called Bart Sanchez, and he sports such sayings scratched into his hat as *Me vale madre*. (The saying is all but indecipherable to the happy shopper: "It matters mother to me.") Along with Bart, there might be a load of piñatas, incredible bargain blankets, and tin Rolexes. At least one of the driver's kids is wearing a sombrero. You've seen this guy a thousand times at the border, waiting in line. He's probably buying six dollars' worth of Chiclets from the insistent street vendors. Someone either cuts in front of him or isn't moving fast enough, or he just feels darned jaunty, so he honks his horn. But to be friendly, he taps out that peculiarly American-sounding five-beat rhythm that we call "shave and a haircut." He might even add the two-beat fillip at the end, which makes it "shave and a haircut, two bits." Hey, everybody knows it. Even Doc Severinsen used to end the Johnny Carson theme with it every night.

However, the Mexican he has honked at does not seem amused. Especially if the Mexican is from Sonora or Chihuahua—a no-nonsense *norteño*. He's craning his neck, glaring at the American. The American, thinking he might bring a smile to his fellow driver, tries it again. The Mexican isn't smiling. In fact, he seems downright insulted. In fact—oh my God—here he comes!

The door jerks open, and in front of his squealing kids and his horrified wife, the American catches five rapid punches on the point of his chin.

Why?

The answer lies in the complexity and creativity of Mexican cussing. The rhythm of "shave and a haircut" translates in Spanish as *Chinga tu madre*. If we add the pleasant "two bits," it's an even worse Mexican insult. Then you're saying *Chinga tu madre, cabrón*. You've called the guy a son of a bitch, for good measure.

This is a linguistic border survival guide. Of all the fascinating developments of the no-man's-land called the border, one of the richest is language. For all the whining Californians do about encroaching Mexicans ("wetbacks" turned to "illegals" turned to "undocumented workers" turning back to "wets"), it's the Mexicans who have wrestled with the glacier of English pressing down all across the borderlands. Any Spanish-lover must be aware of the weird linguistic meteors pocking the surface of Español: *troc* or *troca* for "truck," the dreaded *bistek* for "steak," the amusingly literal *perro caliente* (heated canine) for "hot dog," the elegantly Latinized *hamburguesa* for "hamburger," the peculiar choice of *French* (pronounced with mighty verve but no success as *Frreycch*) for "poodle."

I still remember a bemused Mexican newscaster trying to

figure out a new product, 7UP, on his show. He finally called it *Siete-Ooop*. Mexicans ultimately gave in and call it *un Seven*.

This leads to gentle linguistic jokes that are difficult to translate. I'll try. When something is for sale, the "For Sale" sign in Spanish says *Se Vende*. Hence, fruit sellers will put up a sign that says *Se Vende Piña* or *Se Vende Sandía*. Read a different way, however, with the emphasis shifted, the sign could be said to read *Seven de Piña*. A 7UP *of* pineapple. In other words, a pineapple or watermelon 7UP. Newcomers are fooled into believing they can order a coconut 7UP, and everybody has a hearty laugh at their expense.

As has often been mentioned, the border adds such intimate proximity to the situation that attempts to work alien words into the vocabulary are simply overwhelmed by the rapid-fire assault of language. A phrase that gained wild popularity in the orphanages around Tijuana in the early 1980s, for example, was "Whassamattawichu?" That was followed by "Whazjouname!"

Spanglish is shorthand, a pidgin language that is like a rope ladder. The building's burning down, and we don't have time to check our Larousse bilingual dictionary. We have business and conversation and arguments and deals to attend to. Not only words but concepts have to flow.

"Junkyard" is *yonke*, "muffler" is *mofle*, "bike" is *baica*, "surfer" is *surfo*, the Rolling Stones are *los Rolling*, "rock and roll" is *rocanrol*, "wife" is *waifa*, "cake" is *quéqui*, and "pie" is still *pie*, though that is spelled the same as the word for "foot."

Recently overheard on Tijuana radio, an enthusiastic announcer with twelve pints of reverb thrown on his voice, apparently driven to orgasmic excitement at the prospect of fried chicken, screamed, "Kay-tooky Friiiize Shee-kenzzzz!!!"

□ □ □ □

My father had a hard time with this baffling gringo language. He, like many Mexican immigrants, fretted over concepts and constructs. "When I go to the bathroom," he asked me once, "how can I be 'taking a piss'? I don't *take* a piss, I *leave* a piss. Am I taking the piss *to* the bathroom?"

Americans going into Mexico are similarly baffled. To us, a tuna is a fish. To a Mexican, a tuna is a prickly pear. An *atún* is a fish.

Missionaries are often caught up short in the area of Cross-Border Communications 101. I remember a well-meaning missionary chatting with a gang of orphanage boys, utterly confused about why they were laughing hysterically every time he said anything. If you decide to go tend to the tykes in an *orfa*, you should remember that they are like any other prisoners—bored. Lots of time on their hands. Lots of time to think. And these boys had maneuvered their victim into a seemingly innocent discussion about breakfast.

"How do you like your *huevos?*" they asked.

"*¡Oh, mucho!*" he enthused in his broken Spanish, his accent making the assault even funnier. "*¡Me gusta mucho los huevos! ¡Deliciosos y grandes!*" Which, of course, secretly meant "I love testicles so much! Yummy big balls!"

"And," the gigglers delved, "do you ever eat chorizo?"

"*¡Oh, sí!*"

"*¿Chorizo grande?*"

"*Sí. ¡Me gusta mucho chorizo!*"

How big is this chorizo? they wanted to know. Eight inches? Ten?

He held up his hands, thinking they were pleased that he loved Mexican sausage so much, being a wild and crazy guy, demonstrating a twelve-incher and saying, "Mmm!"

It should be painfully obvious that our Bible-teacher had just confessed to a raging lust for twelve inches of erect penis.

One night at Pastor Von's church, I was taken into an office by a "hip" youth pastor about to insert two busloads of blond Orange County Young Republican Christianity into Tijuana. He wanted to know what to expect in the way of abusive language. "Don't be shy," he said. "We're both grown men." He had a notebook. "Hit me," he said.

I felt a bit odd, cussing at a pastor.

"What do you want to know?" I said.

"Pussy," he whispered. "How do they say pussy?"

"You're kidding."

He smiled.

"*Panocha*," I said. "Which is a candy."

"Candy!"

"Right."

"That's not hateful!"

"Well," I said, "in terms of rude comments about women's anatomy, I suppose it's less vile than English words. But I wouldn't call it respectful, either."

He scribbled.

"Yeah!" he said. He looked up and nodded at me. "Bitch," he said. "You know. Asshole. How do they say it? How do they say fuck? How do the Mexicans say fuck, like 'Fuck you, gringo asshole? Give me your pussy, gringo bitch.' "

His pen hovered over the page, and his eyes gleamed with a joy like that of Christmas morning. Outside the door, his girls and boys slept on the floor, dreaming of saving souls. I stared at him, and he leaned foward eagerly, ready to write.

"Go for it," he said.

Okay, Reverend.

Mother is a dangerous area for comment in Mexico. What every gringo should know about Mexico is that nobody messes with our moms. And every one of our moms, it goes without saying, is a virgin. So you'd better not suggest copulation of any sort.

Because of this, it might be safer to mention someone's *mamá* ("mommy") than their *madre* (the actual word for "mother.") *Madre* carries with it the implicit *chinga tu*. You have to be awfully close to mention someone's *madre* without there being trouble. *Cabrón*, for example, is much less charged than *tu madre* ("yo' mama"). Like Australians calling each other "bastard," Mexican men tend to refer to each other as *cabrón* all the time. Listen to them at the bars in TJ: it's *cabrón* this and *cabrón* that. However, a terse *"Tu madre, cabrón"* tends to be the introductory statement to a flurry of punches and bottles flying.

Cabrón can be seen as a noun *("Tú, cabrón")*, an adjective *("Eso está cabrón")*, or a verb *("Estoy encabronado")*.

Then there's the ever-handy *ni madre*. Literally, this means "not mother." The "fuck," of course, is strongly implied. Since there is no object—it's not really anybody's particular mother being discussed—this phrase is considered strong but not necessarily deadly. It is a way to say no emphatically.

"Do you want to go to jail?"

"¡Ni madre!"

(Don't say this to a cop, by the way, unless you *do* want to go to jail.)

Since *ni madre* is such a strongly obscene quip, you might hear bowdlerized versions, like the nonsensical *ni papas*. Yes, it means "not potatoes."

You will recall another permutation, the Bart Sanchez *Me vale madre*. A rude way of saying, "Dear boy, I simply couldn't care less."

Another form of mother appears in the lascivious, appreciative comment *mamacita* ("little mama"). Men say this to women. Curiously, both feminists and fundamentalists have curbed this practice, since both camps chafe at the implication, which is, basically, "You cute little thing, I'm going to deliver a load of manhood to you." Dimwits who think they're pretty sharp make wordplay with *mamacita* and say instead *mamasota*, which means "great big mama," but actually implies "You have ten times the sex appeal of a *mamacita.*"

A word you might mistake for a mom-derivative is *mamón*. This word means "sucker." It implies actually sucking, either breasts or penises. Sucking a breast here is not macho but insulting; ultimately, it means you're babyish. Mexican men will tell each other, *"No seas mamón"*—don't be a sucker.

Also there is the anachronistic use of *madre* to denote something really good. You will hear a Mexican announce something is *"A toda madre."* The best I can do with this is "at total mother."

As you can surmise by now, the use of *madre* makes the term rude and unacceptable for general public consumption. You'll never hear one of the slick variety-show hosts on Spanish cable saying, "Julio Iglesias—that song was at total mother!" The polite way to say it is *a todo dar*, "at total give," "at ultimate deliver." It reminds me of Arsenio Hall urging us to "give it up." *A todo dar* is quite metaphysical, when you think about it. One is hard-pressed, by the way, to find out whether "at total give" or "at total mother" came first.

There is another interesting way to handle this question. It has worked its way up to us from Mexico City. You simply say *padre* ("father"). If you like it, you just say, "It's father."

"¿Cómo te gusta el Sting?"

"¡Es padre!"

Apparently we haven't yet found fathers to be as obscene as mothers. Or at least they're not as highly charged.

If you really like something, it's *padrísimo*. This would

translate as "superfather," or "fathermost," or perhaps "ultra-fatheritious."

"*¿Cómo te gustan los New Kids on the Block?*"

"*¡Son padrísimos!*"

Meanwhile, back on the mother front, there's another phrase that is cunning and baffling, and some philosopher should tackle it. That phrase is *No tiene madre*, "It/he/she has no mother." It doesn't seem to be obscene, but *madre* could imply a little nastiness. For some reason, it is used to suggest something so good as to be without further description. Say, the ultimate *mamasota*. Some cad, writhing in ecstasy at the memory of a woman, would say, "*¡Esa vieja no tiene madre!*" ("That old woman—broad, actually—has no mother!" Warning: *vieja* is even ruder than *mamasota*, and women all over Mexico resent its use. Oddly, when you've been married for a while, it becomes a term of endearment. Men often call their wives *viejita*).

It seems curious that in a culture as mother-crazy as Mexico, something with no mother would be prized above all others. Perhaps it's that the woman—or movie or horse or job or cigar or boxer—in question is so transcendent as to have apparently descended from heaven. Perfection incarnate.

All these mothers tend to have sons and daughters.

One could write an entire book about being the child of some obscenity in Mexico—or at least a chapter (as Octavio Paz did in *Labyrinth of Solitude*). By now, you can easily see that *hijo/a de tu madre* ("son/daughter of your mother") is dreadfully insulting and should lead to a sound thrashing for the fool who said it to you. This can be augmented, depending on your desire for bodily damage, to florid heights: *hijo de tu chingada madre* ("son of your fucked mother"). There is also *hijo de tu pinche madre* ("son of your goddamn or low-life or fucking mother," depending on your outlook).

Hijo de puta pleasantly suggests you are a son of a whore. A variation of this is the terse *puta madre* ("whore mother"). This is not especially personal. It is a kind of cry against the world. A bellow of astonishment.

My godfather, for example, was fond of this phrase. We'd be watching wrestling on Saturday afternoon. The Destroyer would pull a foreign object out of his trunks and rake it across Pedro Morales's eyes, blinding him. My godfather would shout, "*¡Puta madre!*" Consider it to be a terse way to say, "By gum, this twist of fate is beyond my immediate comprehension!"

Finally, there is the most existential of all Mexican parental curses. It is a curse so bleak, so cold, that it denotes a vast cultural despair more than a juicy dirty word. It is *hijo de la chingada*. "Son of the fuck" (or "son of the *fucked*").

Think of it. In this one phrase is the entire sad history of Mexico. Blood and torment, conquest and failure and rape. (If, as some historians suggest, the *mestizos* who populate Mexico today are the product of the rape of Indian women by European invaders, this curse becomes even more apt.)

When a Mexican is at the end of his rope with you, when his rage and despair have led him to the brink, he calls you *hijo de la chingada*. It is a final, deadly thing to say.

You will find too, if you listen long enough, that Mexicans who turn philosophical invariably tell each other that they are all *hijos de la chingada*. No gringo could ever enter into that solitude. It is a darkness borne with some perverse pride, but it is ultimately damning and tragic.

We are alone. We are abandoned. You do not belong here. We Mexicans—and we alone—are the bastard sons of the fuck.

Think about it the next time you honk your horn.

Borderland Blues:
Six Impressions

Uno: They

They come across the wires in the dark. We walk through their gates on the same night. They dream of our beds, our cars, our clothing. We eat the fruits they pick for us—our salads are washed in their sweat, our strawberries and tomatoes and cotton are passed to us by their fingers. They stare at us through the fence and wonder what our problem is. We keep our doors locked to them, and we let them feed us, and when we're through with them, we pay men in Jeeps to throw them out. We send our losers to their town to entertain themselves. We pass each other on the way, and we never look into each other's eyes.

Early evening, as daylight turned violet-gray and the sea horizon torched copper, I stood at the end of E Street in Chula Vista. Chula Vista (the Precious View) is one of the little scraps of town between San Diego and Tijuana—a buffer zone consisting of National City, Nestor, Imperial Beach, Chula Vista, and San Isidro, the whole region oddly flattened by the pressure of the twins above and below it.

Cutting through it all is the massive flow of Interstate 5 in the west and 805 in the east. There are many ways across the line for "wetbacks" (an odd name for people who don't have to swim across the Rio Grande to get here—maybe they're wet only with blood). Those who don't get out of Tijuana through Colonia Libertad or by being smuggled by car often get trapped by 5's concrete river. It flows dead west along the Mexican border, then veers north and heads all the way up the West Coast. The Border Patrol has come to count on the freeway to siphon the wetbacks along the coast, in a thin strip easily patrolled by helicopter. They get trapped in the saltbogs, the brackish swamps, the navy yards and slag heaps that run from the border to San Diego. Often at night they try to run across the lanes of traffic, and they are run down.

I was in front of Anthony's Fish Grotto restaurant, poking around for no obvious reason. A helicopter cut in a bit closer on its fly-by, checking to see what this gringo-looking fool with a notebook was doing down here. I can imagine one of the agents saying, Some sort of reporter. Looking to get shot, I guess. I wonder if they thought of me as a drive-by poet.

E Street dead-ends at the edge of Anthony's parking lot. Across the street from the restaurant is a weed-choked lot with the foundation of a house in it. Beyond the dead end is a farm, and this property spills into the Deep South swamps of San Diego Bay. Near here, a colony of sea turtles has immigrated into the hot-water ponds off the electric company's big turbines. Apparently the steaming effluent mimics the tropical tides of the Caribbean. Sea World officials, zookeepers, and animal control officers regularly stop them and check them for papers; the bright-hued plastic tags punched into their fins pass for turtle green cards. The Mark of the Aquatic Beast.

□ □ □ □

Another road runs at right angles to E, and the two form a dusty T. The arm of this T that runs north, toward San Diego, ends abruptly at the edge of a briny area of tide marshes and bogs. It is barricaded. Parallel to this road is a set of rusted train tracks. It was here, along this road, that I found myself among the remnants of what seemed a lost race, the spoor of courage and desperation.

I walked north along the closed road, veering around a barricade that kept cars from the area. Grass had worked its way through the blacktop, cracking and lifting triangular pieces of it. There was a ditch on the left, and every few yards there were clumps of tired pine trees. I could see the abandoned rail line through the trees. There were peeling PRIVATE PROPERTY signs posted all along the edge of the farm. A crumpled pair of blue jeans in the road. The silence. A cottontail broke from cover in the crumbling foundation and ran in panicked jags. The river-hiss of 5 to my right underlined the quiet. A blue-and-yellow CAT baseball cap was dangling from a twig.

It was so lonely out there. Not restive, not solitary; *lonely*. I began to feel sad, then furtive. I was convinced somebody was watching me. I imagined a rifle scope trained on my back. I wanted to hide.

It was like a smell. I looked around for its source and suddenly got a hunch. I cautiously stepped down one of the little banks into the ditch between the road and the tracks. I crawled under a pine.

They'd been there.

There were cardboard sleeping mats, small white roses of crumpled paper, flat liquor bottles, dry scat. All along the ditch there were hidey-holes burrowed out among the roots and pine needles, dens scraped out between a flood of cars and a dead railway.

I moved into the hole. There was dust all over the cardboard mats. It had clearly been a while since anyone hid here. Had the people been arrested? Had this spot been compromised, discovered by la migra, and rendered permanently unsafe? Perhaps they made it north. Maybe locals found them and made sport of them. (The Ku Klux Klan had been patrolling the region, "assisting" the U.S. government in the roundup of unwanted humans.)

A broken bottle of Mexican beer. Magazine pages smashed into petrified stools. I could feel the pulse of these men, lying here, hiding night after night. Who, I wondered, who? I might have known them. I might have fed them the week before they came here.

One stained mattress. A shattered TV set on the tracks. There was nothing left here. Not a voice. I felt watched by shadows as I climbed out, hurried away from the traces of sorrow downwind of the city.

Dos: Mother X

The nun was drinking Mexican beer out of a large glass mug. We were in a border town that will remain nameless; for reasons of her own safety, so will she. I believe her security will not be compromised if I tell you that everyone calls her Mother.

Mother works at a Catholic orphanage on the Mexican side of the border. Many of her charges are the castoffs of whores, addicts, prisoners, vanished illegals, and the disappeared. (In Mexico, an orphan is not necessarily what we in the United States expect. For example, an orphan can be abandoned, or simply poor. Mexico's ever-creative bureaucracy has taken care of the problem of living parents by labeling all the children in these institutions "children with needs.") There is great violence and turmoil on the border, and parents go away. If you were shot tonight, for example, your children could very well find themselves—within days—sleeping under cars. Recruits for the army of hopelessness massing at our frontier.

Unless someone like Mother takes them in.

Earlier in the day, Mother had taken me into her nursery, where a tiny deformed baby girl slept in a crib. Someone had found her in a closed trash can behind a store. The baby was suffering from exposure and dehydration, but Mother and her staff had managed to keep her alive.

Mother touched her head and said, "Precious. What kind of person would throw you away?"

Now we were in a restaurant fixed up to look like an old hacienda, and the waiter was clearly astounded to be serving beer to this elderly nun in full habit.

"Mother," I said, "you don't look like you go out on many dates."

She was wolfing down a platter of beef, and crowed, "Haw! I'm too old for boyfriends!"

Over our beer, Mother told me some details about the difficulties involved in adopting a child from the border.

Corruption is so great that in bribes alone, an American family can be soaked for $20,000 to $40,000 per child. Everywhere, there is an open hand—the orphanage director will want a kickback, the Mexican officials will want theirs, even the Mexican police will show up. The city hall recordkeeper stands to earn a good chunk of money because, incredibly enough, to adopt a child on the border, you must have written and signed permission from both parents.

In other words, you pay.

Mother had two ingenious ways around this. The first, legal way was to have the child transferred to a nunnery in the deep south of Mexico. There, though graft is still pandemic, it doesn't have the virulence associated with fleecing gringos. Consequently, you have a chance to adopt a child for a mere couple of thousand dollars. Or, miraculously, simply to adopt without being victimized at all.

Mother's other, more daring, and highly illegal tactic is much more direct.

It is fairly common for Mexican orphanages to bring children to the United States for weekend visits. They are often invited by churches or such groups as the Shriners, and the kids are treated to visits to zoos or Disneyland or taken on camp-outs. (U.S. immigration officers are usually pretty friendly . . . at least to invited children. You have to be *invited*, though, or all cordiality is called off.)

The orphanage bus will pull into the secondary inspection area at the international border crossing, and an INS officer will board with a complete list of names. He takes the kids out one by one, checks them off, does a head count, looks at your itinerary, and usually sends you off for a fun weekend. Supposedly, the Mexican guards will do the same on your way back in. The Mexicans don't care. They barely look in the windows of the bus, much less board, count heads, sign papers, make reports. No way. They see a nun, a vehicle full of forty or so kids, and they wave it through before anyone can make them do any work.

When Mother's bus gets to its destination, men and women are waiting. These are couples who have applied to adopt from her but who cannot afford the terrible fees, or for any of a number of reasons they cannot arrange the long trip into southern Mexico.

Mother ushers the children to the gates of the zoo. Most of the children. The lucky ones meet their new parents in the shadow of the bus. After a quick prayer and a blessing from Mother, they get in their cars and drive home. Mother says she feels happiest at that moment, watching them drive out of sight. Then, her work done, she walks into the zoo. Hot dogs, cotton candy, the sea lion show, and the elephants. Sunburned, happy, she returns that night and lies down vindicated. Mother X sleeps, free of any sin.

Tres: Felix

Felix was the bad street boy whom everyone hated. Von often talked about loving the unlovable, and Felix was that. He reminded me of a dirty alley cat, all knobby with scars and cat scratches, fur full of oil from the cars he lurked under. And when you petted him, he was as likely to scratch you and spit as to purr.

He was only nine or ten when I met him. He appeared regularly at Abigail's orphanage for baths—though it was his special art to resist being bathed until the last possible minute, and even then he would cuss and shove and parade before the others, making cutting remarks about the other boys' bodies, the fat bellies and the pitiably tiny *pipís*.

He also attended Von's weekly Bible studies, but he resisted these even more strenuously than the baths. He made it very clear that he was there for the doughnuts, the chocolate milk, and the American women. He was the figurehead of a disruptive crew, little dudes with switchblades in their socks and constant insults on their tongues. As Elvis said, "I was born standin' up and talkin' back."

Von proved to be a worthy adversary, though. One night Felix's pals ate all of Von's doughnuts, leaving none for the rest of the children. One of the boys wiped his mouth and sneered.

"Your doughnuts taste like monkey shit," he said.

They laughed wickedly. Felix gave him a *cholo* handshake. I translated.

Von didn't even blink.

He shot back, "Oh? You recognize the taste, do you? You must eat a lot of monkey shit."

The boy paled and stammered as everyone pointed at him and howled.

Felix was scruffy and thin. He had freckles and lighter hair than all the other boys. They called him Llellé. It could have been an insult or a nickname—I never learned what it meant.

He was always picking fights he had no hope of winning. He was not interested in hugs of any kind, unlike the other street kids. If, after Felix had gotten yet another bloody nose, you tried to hug him, you'd get a flurry of rabbit punches to the gut. (After a few years, though, Felix relented; he learned to accept a brotherly arm draped over his shoulder, but it had to be low-key and almost accidental.)

Then one day, for reasons I never figured out, he decided to tell me his story. He took me aside and we talked in the dirt street that ran in front of Abigail's. Inside, they were singing. We sat on a low wall, and he dangled his feet.

Both his parents were dead. They had apparently died in an accident of some kind, and he'd been left with an aunt who resented him at first, then hated him. Felix's aunt beat him regularly, insulted him continually, and often refused to feed

him. Finally she threw him out. The kids in the neighborhood thought he had a home—he had told them he did.

One of his favorite stories was that gas station attendants
had taken him in and he was able to fix any car, do any me-
chanical bit of engineering that came his way. They drank
beer with him, shared women and marijuana with him, and he
even stayed up all night whenever he felt like it, watching
dirty movies and polishing his guns.

The reality was that Felix was sleeping in a pile of used
tires. He lived entirely off the street, stealing and begging and
conning. Still, he refused all help.

One winter Felix got new boots. They were huge, heavy hik-
ing boots. "My mother gave them to me!" he boasted.

I knew this to be impossible, and I assumed them to be
stolen. I kept quiet. However he'd gotten them, I was glad he
had his feet shod—it was bitterly cold in the hills above Tijuana, and at least he had warm feet. Besides, the other boys
were very impressed that Felix's mother would send him such
nice shoes, probably from some fancy city in California.

Something interesting soon happened. I was translating
one of Von's messages to the kids. It was a good one, one of
his greatest hits: you can't see God, but what you can see is
evidence of Him; likewise, you can't see the current of electricity running down a wire, but when the current hits a bulb,
you see the evidence of it. When the bulb lights, you believe
in electricity because it *works*. It's the same with God—you
see His works and you know He *is*.

We were rolling along, and I was looking around as we
talked. Felix was there, feet planted solidly on the floor, new
boots beautiful and heavy. He, of course, was causing all kinds
of trouble, arguing with Von, elbowing his neighbors, making
faces at me. I glanced back at his feet. A toe was showing.

I looked closer. His big toe was sticking out from under the boot, and then I saw a couple of other toes as they curled against the cold cement floor and hid under the shoe leather.

After Von was through, I took Felix outside and said, "Let me see your boot."

"No!"

"Show me!"

"Hell, no!"

I grabbed him. He put up quite a fight, but I got him off the ground and upended him. The boots had no soles. They were simply cast-off leather uppers, and he had gone through the winter essentially barefoot.

He was humiliated and furious that I'd found out. His fabulous boots, the envy of all the other kids, who had taunted him for so long, were a sham.

"Don't you tell anybody!" he demanded.

I took Von aside and had a quiet conference. He slipped me some money, and I took Felix downtown. He acted completely unimpressed by this turn of events. When I asked him if he was happy, he shrugged.

"I don't care," he said.

He managed to insult the shoe store clerks and the entire inventory of the store we'd chosen. I shoved him into a seat, and the saleslady put new boots on his feet and laced them tightly. Felix couldn't show us that he liked them, but he kept glancing at them, turning his foot when he thought we weren't looking.

I took him back up to the barrio, and we punched each other a few times, then he clomped off, bellowing, "Hey, you little punks! Look at what I'm gonna kick your asses with now!"

When I next saw him, Felix was as insufferable as ever. He

was goose-stepping around, crowing about his exploits and showing off the boots.

"My mama sent them, *cabrones!*" he shouted. "She is an actress in the movies, in America!"

Cuatro: Incident at San Antonio

There isn't much to the village of San Antonio.

It is easy to drive past it, thinking there is nothing there but a roadside soda stand. It's a tiny hamlet on a bend in the road in an area of vineyards. There are a couple of houses and two stores, side by side. Near the stores you will see a white-washed adobe wall with a large gate in it and a sign that says, ESTADO 29. It is an orphanage, State Orphanage Number Twenty-nine.

I was taking one of the boys from Twenty-nine to the store; we had to buy some lard for the cook, and I was going to get him a lollipop and a Coke.

Along the side of one of the stores is a wooden bench. Unemployed men sit here all day and drink beer. (It has always seemed a miracle to me that Mexican men, without one cent, produce enough money to get thoroughly drunk.) When we are in the area, working, they stare at us, not sure what to do about it. They clearly think they ought to be heckling us, at the very least. On this day they were busy arguing drunkenly, waggling fingers at each other and standing up to make pronouncements, then sitting back down and crossing their arms with a flourish, like characters out of *Tortilla Flat.*

Suddenly the door of the house behind the store slammed,

and a woman in tight Levi's and a knit sweater appeared in the street. She stood there, glaring at the men.

One of them in particular was apparently the focus of her gaze. He tipped down the bill of his cap, trying to be invisible. That didn't work. He huffed and straightened up and flung his arms out as if exasperated by her nagging. "What do you want?" he sneered, in a ploy obviously intended more for his *compadres* than for her.

They looked quite pleased with him.

She said nothing.

Emboldened, he said, "Answer me!"

Silent, she pulled a set of car keys out of her pocket and held them up for him to see.

He stood.

"Give me those keys!" he ordered.

She turned on her heel and walked away.

"Don't you *ever*," he announced, finger pointing, "walk away from me!"

The drunks were stirring.

She was heading for a car.

"Don't touch that car!"

She touched it: she opened the door.

"I'm telling you to get away from that car!" He took a wobbly step toward her.

The *compadres* were impressed with him, that much was obvious.

"And don't think you're getting inside!"

She got in.

The drunks were mortified.

"*¡Hija de puta!*" he squealed. "I'll kill you! [*¡Te mato!*] Do *not* start that %#$@!*! engine!"

She started the engine and popped it in gear.

He was bright crimson by now.

In slow, threatening cadence, he warned, "Don't. You. DARE. Drive. Away. IN MY CAR!"

She peeled out, splattering him with dirt and pebbles.

The drunks hung their heads, looked away.

We all watched her speed off toward Ensenada. She never slowed down. When the car was a mere wink in the distance, he drew himself up to full height and shouted, "All right! Fine! But don't even *think* about bringing the car back!"

The *compadres* were delighted.

"You told her!" they cried, slapping his back, opening more beers.

He reclaimed his seat among them and smiled.

"The man," he said, sighing, "is always on top. That's just the way it is."

Cinco: Tijuana Trolley

Six-thirty A.M., southbound

He was a little dude with no shirt, no front teeth, a battered Levi jacket, and this design tattooed on his stomach:

There were words etched into his skin at the end of each little line, but I couldn't make them out. I was on my way to work as a teaching assistant for English-as-a-second-language (Mexican) students at a southern county college. That night I was due to join Von to go into Tijuana and translate a sermon.

The short guy swaggered up to the man in the seat next to me and said, "You wanna move this stuff?"

The man shifted his bundle, and the guy sat down and stared at me.

"I just ran all the way from Thirtieth Street!" he said.

"Shee," I said appreciatively, thinking *Don't talk to me*.

"Gotta go to the post office in Chula Vista, off H."

Great, I thought, *my stop*.

"Could of run faster if I didn't have these *steel-toe* workboots." He looked at my foot. "What size you wear?"

I told him.

"Hey," he cried, "that's just my size!"

Brother, I thought, *you are not walking away with my shoes*.

We rode on; he began talking to himself—something about fistfights. Then he asked me, "Is that him?"

"Who?" I said.

"Who's that?" he replied.

The trolley stopped.

"What," he announced, "we run out of gas or sompin?"

This struck him as funny, and he repeated it with laughter mixed in: "Ru-hu-hun outa ga-ha-has!" Then: "I got pive hunnerd dollars at the post office, man, but if I ain't there by eight-thirty, porget it!"

I was noticing his mouth—he was missing teeth, and this had given him a marked case of slack lip. For some reason it was making him replace his *f* sounds with *p* sounds.

When we got off the trolley, he said, "Cheafest ride I ever got!" He patted his empty pockets and smiled. He walked in front of the train and made like he was diving under the wheels. He beamed at the stone-faced driver and did it again. "I wanna end it all!" he shouted at the windshield.

The driver nodded like he heard this at every stop, made the trolley horn quack twice, and pulled away.

He told me he was turning thirty-five in a week.

"Goin to Tijuana," he said. "Get Rosita an a bottle op tequila! Got rolled one time. Shit! Puckin police put a .38 special to my head! Puckin real gun, man. Tol me I'd get three months at La Mesa prison ip I dint give 'em the money. Then I got hit wit my own tequila bottle and kicked down some stairs. Motherpuck! I'm goin *armed* tonight. Takin a little Beretta tucked down in my boot, and I'mo put a couple little holes in somebody. Won't kill nobody"—he pressed the tip of his index finger into his forehead, between his eyebrows— " 'less I get him right here. Twenty-pive caliber. Lookee here, podner." A bulge in his boot. "I had a guy your size wit me too, an he ran away! Chicken! Hey, I ain't gettin killed por no Citizen Watch, I tell ya. Take care, buddy."

He stomped away, bouncing like a superball, bouncing so high off his heels it looked for a moment like he was going to launch himself right off the ground, fly away. Small as an armed sprite. Jolly as Puck.

Seis: Shadow Orphans

We were in the backlands, northeast of Ensenada, about one hundred miles from San Diego. There had been talk of an orphanage in the low hills, but nobody had much to say about it. It was somewhat akin to Colonel Kurtz's compound— along the road some spoke of it, but no one had gone there. It was a myth, and when I heard tell of it, the stories were dark and witchy. Still, the directors of the two nearest orphanages were both staunch Christians, and one thing you learn about Christian orphanage directors in Mexico, they each think the next one is evil incarnate. Dead-baby stories, mysterious-tall-black-man-doing-eerie-things-at-night stories, abuse stories, witchcraft and demonology stories, racketeering-false-Christian-idolatry-con-artist-alcoholism-pornography stories.

The director of one of the orphanages said, "Go see for yourself. You won't believe it. But be careful."

Careful. That seemed an odd thing to say about an orphanage.

"They have a gun," he said. "They will shoot."

Generally speaking, in spite of this warning, I knew that orphanages were not hotbeds of crime and danger. Most of the *orfanatorios* along the Mexican border are religious in nature, not only Catholic but evangelical and Pentecostal as well. In fact, I'd wager that the born-again operations outnumber the Catholic outfits three to one.

The *orfas* varied wildly, from sub-Dickensian dens of horror to gleaming, gringofied Bible schools. And then there was the strange subset of orphanages, the private, in-home *orfas*. For some reason, people would suddenly decide to take in needy and abandoned children. Whether they were led by the spirit, by greed, or by some nebulous personal agenda, we can never know. They got no money for doing this, though their instant connection to whatever missionary group was working the region had direct positive effects for them, it cannot be denied. These *orfas* would immediately make themselves available for Bible studies by the missionaries. Thus the house would become a kind of neighborhood centerpiece, a focus for lots of action, and the director of the *orfa* would become an instant authority. Kind of the mayor of the barrio.

Extra food and clothing would start to come in. Special consideration from the missionaries, too, in the form of extra doughnuts, watches, shoes, extra beans, whatever was on hand to keep the Bible study room available. And then occasionally there was a motherlode of stuff to be handed out to the neighbors. With the directors suddenly sitting on rice, beans, Pampers, whatever, they were transformed from mayor of the barrio to Pope of the barrio. In a world of little personal power, a little power goes a long way.

Along with no obvious educational or philosophical or political or social agenda, these private *orfas* had no official documentation. It was not uncommon for raids to descend on these houses, and the children were hustled out the door into a future that was uncertain, at best. One unaffiliated orphanage in the Tijuana hills was found out by the local cops, who gave the director a week to come up with a heavy fine (read: bribe). When she couldn't pay, the children were rounded up and marched into the night—at gunpoint. It seems that the cops were out their money, but they were going to teach the director to respect the law. And next time they caught her, she'd pay.

What happened to the kids? One boy started living under a car. I never heard anything about the girls again.

Although some of these unaffiliated *orfas* rely on missionary goodness, many do not. Often they are better run than the big church-sponsored orphanages. If poor, which most of them are, they are often family homes, and at the very least, the children live with a figurehead mother and father. Some of the children are galley slaves, it's true: they are forced to do all the chores, to tend pigs and chickens and goats, to run errands, mop floors, do dishes, wash clothes.

However, these little communes—usually consisting of six or ten extra kids crammed into the back bedrooms of a house on a hidden-away dirt alley, along with the host family—are far better than the street. Some of these kids are experiencing a "normal" life for the first time. Baths, regular meals, school, beds, education, and the Bible. Pets. Television. It could be worse. It usually is.

Weirdness blossoms all over the world, however. It creeps up from dark corners like fungus, and it's a dark gray color, and it smells. We have all seen a news report about some inexplicable yahoo out in the country with a kennel full of dead, frozen, and starving dogs. Or a grandmother who is discovered living in a one-room apartment with eighty-four starved cats. Some people collect children. Some people are fulfilling an agenda that cannot be translated, codified, or understood.

We drove out a narrow dirt road. I was with a young buck named Rick. He had grown up under Pastor Von, had lived in the jungles of South America, and more than many of the workers in the group he prided himself on being unflappable. If anyone on the Mexico crew had seen it all, it was Rick and me.

The day was dark and cold; the rains had recently stopped, and the land was still saturated. Normally, the high land around the Ensenada harbor is warm, dry, and pleasant. We were in a valley housing vineyards and small farms; it was full of goldenrod and tall grasses, and trees followed the course of a creek that meandered under stone bridges. The deep soil was red clay, and several men of the valley made their money by digging this mud and drying it in wooden flats; curved roof tiles were laid over a long pole, with newspaper between the slats of clay. The brickmakers took long machetes and sliced them apart like bread.

We had to drive only about a mile past the brickmakers to find the orphanage. The road twisted through scrub oak in loose switchbacks that would have been impassable with another inch of rain. There was a sharp left, a small rise, and we stopped. I wasn't sure at first what I was seeing. Was this the place?

Slanting gray fenceposts, a drooping wire gate. No dogs. A low hillside scattered with trash, broken machines.

There were no buildings, no dorms. The slope was denuded, and a rundown house huddled at the top, low-roofed and seemingly hand-built. The old whitewash was flecked off the boards, and a dead washing machine sat against the yawning screen door—it could have been the front door or the back door. The silence felt wet, heavy, and muffling.

Scattered around this house was what looked to be more junk—camper shells, cardboard and wooden boxes. I was certain we had taken a wrong turn. I turned to say something to Rick.

Then the children began to come out.

They came up from under the camper shells. The back windows swung up, and two, three, four children crawled into the gray light. I could see them heaving themselves out of . . . *burrows*, some kind of pits, foxholes, dug into the hillside and covered with this wreckage.

"Nice playground," Rick said.

They stood there staring at us. They didn't scamper, shout, or run. Some of their clothes were tattered, the rest were typical orphanage fare: old blue jeans, battered corduroys, striped T-shirts, cast-off little dresses. All of the children were dirty, ashen, with mud caked on knees, hands black. Staring. Not talking among themselves, not pointing, not screaming and laughing and yelling for candy.

I got out of the van, but none of them made a move. Rick sat behind the wheel and said, "What the —?" I waved. They watched.

"Where is the director?" I asked.

They pointed at the house.

I walked up there, puzzled and apprehensive. Behind me, the entire compound was silent. Rick kept the engine running. "Don't get shot," he called. This, for us, was a funny joke.

I was chuckling as I started to knock on the dark screen door. I realized there was a form behind it. It was a woman, barely visible through the mesh.

"What do you want?" she said. "I have a gun."

I showed her my hands. I told her we worked with orphanages. I told her my name. I told her I worked with *el famoso Hermano Von*.

"I know who you are."

I asked her if they needed anything.

"No."

"Food?"

"Nothing. Go away."

"Would you like us to stop here in the future? Bring food or clothes? Help you build—"

"*Nada*. Nothing. Go away."

I looked around.

"The children," I said. "Where do they live?"

She gestured at the camper shells, the boxes. Said, "In the dormitories," as if I were a fool. "Now go, and don't come back."

I walked back to the van through the ranks of silent children. Small dogs had finally come out too. They were as quiet as the kids. No barking, no tail-wagging. They sat in the dirt by the children and seemed to be staring at us too.

"Weird," I said.

"Let's get out of here," Rick said.

We backed out, and the kids started to go back into their holes. Rick started to speed. We slammed around the corners, scaring crows and kicking up mud. I rolled down my window and breathed in the clean air.

"What," he finally said, "*was* that?"

I shrugged.

I knew I would never return.

In a week or two, it would seem like a strange dream.

Just give it a year, I thought. If you don't look in your journal, you'll forget all about it. Never happened. Turn the page.

In the Wet

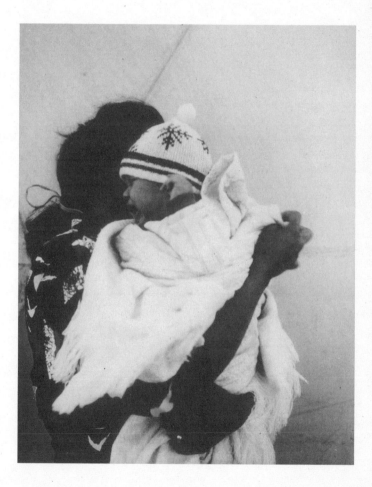

Like many small Mexican towns, Guadalupe had several vaguely eccentric details that were endearing, lending it an air of minor surrealism. It was built on the floodplain of a river. The small Protestant church on the northern edge of town had fat black bats hanging from its rafters. If you were to attend church there, the bats would suddenly take umbrage at the barrage of hymns tearing through the joint, and they'd drop and flutter, dive-bombing the flock like cast-out demons. And the Domecq vineyards were cheek by jowl with an orphanage-ranch for deaf-mute children. Rumor had it that Russians were everywhere, farming and making wine, and this accounted for the occasional blond or redheaded child. Once, at the small Pemex station on the road out of town, the attendants and I stood and watched in awe as an idling Jeep popped into gear for no apparent reason and drove down the road. We hurried into the street and watched it roll off at a steady five mph until it disappeared around a gradual curve.

Near this station was the dirt road through town. It ran past small ugly shops—a hopeless beauty salon, a shoemaker's shop with a jaunty hand-painted red sign. Dust, dogs, kids, and old trucks; sometimes a horse. That was about it for downtown Guadalupe. Then the river came along one night and wiped Guadalupe off its bed like a smear of dirt. We couldn't believe it when we finally made our way through the devastated backcountry to deliver food to orphanages. We'd been in town the week before, stopping for gas, for a taco or a Popsicle. Seven days later, there was nothing but mud and a few cars parked at the edge of the mud, all the drivers shaking their heads just like us. We'd look at each other and raise our shoulders and open our mouths and say nothing. The effect of the flood was simple and absolute.

The flooding ate the ground in massive cuts and crevices. The toll road from Tijuana to Ensenada was washed out. We knew the backcountry way, and on our first journeys into the flood-lands we used it. About halfway to Ensenada, there was an orphanage built in a wide valley, and the entire compound was buried under two or three feet of mud. Helicopters were hovering above the ground, filming missionaries shoveling muck.

Much of this road was hilltop- and plateau-running, so the drives were uneventful for the most part. But when the road dipped into canyons or valleys, there was always some sign of destruction. It was horribly exciting for people who had never seen mass devastation before. Some of us had trouble believing it was real. It was not uncommon to find a car upside-down in a tree. Once we saw three cars upended and hung in trees like ornaments on a single right curve. I almost expected Mad Max to drive through.

Near the end of the inland route, near El Sauzal above Ensenada, the bridges were cracked and listing. The government opted for the traditional Mexican response to crisis: send in a hundred seventeen-year-old soldiers with machine guns to storm around ordering drivers on and off the road. We watched a school bus full of *Jeezuss Iz Lord-ah!* teens from some Orange County church stop praising God when they realized six guns were pointed at them and they were being led across a broken bridge above a raging stream. We were all either being rescued or about to be arrested and lined up against a wall for being stupid enough to drive around in a flood.

The interior was wiped out. Hung along the road running from Ensenada to Tecate, small settlements were far from help and seemingly forgotten. At the worst of it, there was no way help could have gotten to them. Tecate was cut off from the backcountry by an instant volunteer river that rushed out of the hills behind the town; the Guadalupe flood took care of any passage from Ensenada. The village of San Antonio was built along the banks of a small stream that had become a jet of coffee-and-cream water. It came upon them so fast and hard that it didn't even flood their homes, just tore in the front doors and blew out the back windows. The muddy houses all had saturated curtains hanging outside the broken windows. Dogs and pigs dotted the mud like soft stones.

Farther up the road, there were places, isolated for a week or more, where the families had run out of food. Dead cattle and pollution and stagnant water had begun minor typhus and diphtheria plagues. More than once we'd drive over a wobbly S.O.S. painted in the middle of the highway, the farmers and brickmakers hoping some plane or helicopter would come.

We were trying to get to an orphanage in the Las Palmas valley, southwest of Tecate. Like Guadalupe, Las Palmas has a small river running through it. The river is usually dry, its sandy bed a wide place in the valley bottom for wild boys to spin out in their hot rods. The orphanage was built on its bank, up far enough to avoid being swept away. But when winter rains came, the place was cut off by water.

The river was capricious in its effects. One year it carried off a house perched at its edge, leaving only a washing machine. It also brought marvelous objects down from the hills and visited them upon the orphanage. A statue of the Virgin Mary appeared on the bank one morning, come from some distant homestead. Shortly thereafter, an apparently pre-Columbian statue of a goddess or a mortal woman squatting and seemingly preparing to give birth appeared in the flood. But my personal favorite was a 1960 Comet station wagon. Pale blue, it was driven down the length of the river by the floodtide. For some reason, the car turned itself around in a kind of bobbing U-turn right in front of the orphanage and its rear end sank into the quicksand, and then the water cut a bank all around it and abandoned it.

The Comet rose from the riverbed after the flood like a small iceberg. Much of its rear end was buried in the sand, and its hood and left front fender rose at an angle. Enough of the driver's compartment was free of the sand to allow the kids to crawl in and pretend they were driving. Everybody from the orphanage shuffled out regularly and gawked. Surely this was the strangest gift a river had ever brought anyone. We often wondered if a driver was buried somewhere deeper in the car. I could imagine him in the back, curled on one side, packed tight in the soil.

We got to the valley at night. It was flooded. Drowned cows had been shoved to the hollows of the hills by tractors, and their damp skulls formed mounds that peered over the cacti. It had stopped raining, and the water seemed to have topped off. It was so dark, though, that there was no way to see the river bottom to creep across. We were driving a Blazer and three vans. Somebody had to be willing to get out and wade through with a flashlight, directing the vehicles.

I don't know what got into me!

I had my pants rolled up as far as I could get them, and I was barefoot. The water was extremely shallow, and I was sticking to the sandbanks. I shone a path with the flashlight about every fifteen feet, and the vehicles would inch farther along. Suddenly I saw a wide sandbar running right up to shore, and I signaled them on, lighting the way. They sped by, and I ran across after them. The water wasn't only shallow, it was cold. So cold that my feet were completely numb. I couldn't even feel the bottom. As I ran, I sensed the most curious thing happening to my right foot. There was a solid punch in the sole, and I thought of an awl breaking through leather.

I almost fell down when I hit the shore—I had a six-inch branch stuck flat against the sole of my foot. One of the drivers came back and looked at it. Fortunately, my foot was still numb. "Hmm," he said. He grabbed the branch like a handle and tugged. A two-inch thorn came out of my foot. It looked like a magic trick.

The children at the orphanage cheered me up.

We drank hot cocoa and ate doughnuts. We built a fire. We sat close together and watched it rain. The rain should have been a warning to us.

Damn, my foot hurt! I was already cranky when we got to the river and realized it had risen. There was no way I was going back out there. The first van started across and hit a sink-hole and sank up to its fenders. The second managed to make it across, turn around, and come back to attach a tow line. When it tried to pull the first van out, it dug itself into the riverbed. Water was curling off the sides of the vans at door level. The third van entered the water and stalled out immediately.

Suddenly headlights illuminated us from a distance. A loud supercharged engine could be heard making its way toward us from the cattle ranch next door to the orphanage. From behind the scrub along the bank, a searchlight beam flashed across the water, lighting each stranded vehicle. The faces within looked as pale as fish in a tank when the beam hit them.

A big pickup appeared. A Mexican rancher with a big cowboy hat hung his head out the window.

"What's up?" he called.

It was obvious what was up. We pointed.

"How many vans?"

"Three."

"How about the Blazer?"

"It's okay."

"How much will you pay me to pull all three vans out?"

Negotiations proceeded thusly:

RANCHER: I have a tractor. How much for a tow?

US: How much do you want?

RANCHER: How much will you pay?

US: Well, that depends on how much you want.

RANCHER: You go first.

US: Forty dollars.

RANCHER: Be back in a minute.

Soon a set of lights that looked exactly like a UFO from *Close Encounters* bore down on us. Our hero arrived high atop a huge John Deere.

"It looks like a spaceship!" I called.

"Show me some cash," he called down, rubbing his fingertips together in the universal sign for *dinero*.

I showed him the money.

"Climb up here," he said.

There was no seat up there. I perched on the fender of the tractor as we rolled into the water. He revealed many secrets: his love of his tractor, his difficulty with its gearbox, his problem with liquor, his supper, his pickup. ("How do you get the engine to sound so loud?" I asked. "It needs a tune-up," he replied.)

"You just came from the orphanage?" he asked.

"Yes," I said, clinging to the fender.

"You carry a lot of money around with you," he said.

I had visions of a tractor ambush, so I said, "Well, at Christmas we carry some money. You know—you have to carry money for Christmas."

Then the women in our group caught his eye.

"Who's that?" he asked.

I told him.

"She's good-looking. Is she a virgin?"

"What?" I said.

"Is she a virgin?"

"I don't know."

"Lots of women in your group."

"Yes."

"Are *they* virgins?"

This seemed overwhelmingly important to my friend.

"I don't know," I said.

"You should give me one of them," he offered. "I could take her back to the ranch and warm her right up for you!"

This really cracked him up.

By the time we got the vans across, we'd been at it for over an hour. We were all shivering and soaked. We unhooked the tractor's tow chain and watched our savior motor back across the river. The entire valley was full of shallow water. The flood had knocked the lights out. We drove carefully where we figured the road had been, aiming for the midpoint between rows of trees. The headlights turned the trees gray and the water black.

There was a school about a mile or two down the road, and the floodwaters had come along and knocked its bus over on its roof.

We were all exhausted. I still had to get to a hospital to get a battery of shots for the various microbial invaders currently partying inside my foot. We were heading north, to Tecate, and hoping the water had receded enough for us to get through town. It was just another mile to the highway, then across the small bridge crossing the river—if the bridge wasn't washed out.

We inched through the water, the front of our van pushing up a crest like a boat. We were just at the highway, finally, and driving up to the blacktop, out of the water, hoping to get home, when the battery shorted out and we rolled to a silent, dark stop. All we could hear was the endless rush and chuckle of the water slowly rising and erasing the entire landscape.

The Bald Monkey
and Other Atrocities

I had popped my knee—it sounded like chicken bones break-ing when it went, and a sheet of white pain blanked me out. I fell to my side and gasped. Several of the missionaries carted me off to a clinic. Even after six months, my leg was weak, the knee very tender. Sometimes I still limped, especially on days like today, riding three hundred miles through the backcoun-try, in and out of valleys in the central highlands of northern Baja. Hours spent cramped in a van with other people, then hauling hundred-pound sacks of food into orphanages, made the leg stiff and sore.

I was walking around the end of a low barbed-wire fence, thinking I'd try to climb over it on my way back. The kids at the orphanage had run up to me, shouting something about a monkey on the roof of the school next door. I couldn't believe it—I'd seen a lot of things at the orphanages, but never a monkey.

We climbed up the outside of the building on wooden lad-ders, and there on the roof was a monkey. He was little and black, but skin-black; all his hair was gone. It was a brutally hot day, around noon. The monkey was screaming. He had a chain around his neck, and a boy had hold of the end of it and was swinging him around, choking him. I slapped the chain from the boy's hand, and the monkey thumped to the roof. The kids all stopped laughing and stared at me in disbelief. The monkey ran to my ankle and climbed up my leg, chittering.

"Get out of here!" I said to them. "Go on! Leave him alone!"

They backed away and filtered down off the roof. The monkey climbed up into my arms and wrapped his tail around my biceps. He put out a hand and stroked my jaw, putting his lips out in a kiss, cooing. My leg was still stiff, so I had trouble sitting down. There was a post in the middle of the roof—his chain was attached to it. I put my back against it and slid down. The cement was hot; the post was the only source of shade up there. The monkey reclined in my arms. He was trembling, his skin as hot and sticky as overheated vinyl.

The countryside was burned yellow by the sun. In the distance, a truck raised a plume of dust. Smoke rose from the hills.

I'd blow in the monkey's face. He would close his eyes, tilt back his head, and stick out his tongue. His tail was thin and surprisingly muscular; it never let go of its grip on my arm. He liked my whiskers; he ran his finger across my cheeks.

He was panting. There was a can of water. I gave him one drop, then another. I used my body to shield him from the sun. The truck's dust hung in the air, unmoving. It looked like trees.

In about an hour, a big boy climbed onto the roof, followed by a flock of little kids. The monkey was his. When he reached for it, the monkey tried to bite him. It scrambled up my neck and screamed when they tried to pull it off. The boy dragged it away from me with the chain. As I climbed down, I could hear it shrieking, the chain clanking on the cement.

I wanted to get away from there. One of the orphanage

boys climbed on my back. I decided to step over the barbed-
wire fence instead of going around it. My knee gave out halfway across, and I fell back into the wire. It tore my thigh
open, and blood spurted out.

The boy helped me across the fence with a spooked look on
his face. Little boys always stare at blood like it's a miracle.

I went into the bathroom where Pastor Von was bathing
the orphanage boys.

"Drop your pants," he said.

We could see the fat inside my leg through the cut. "Looks
good," Von said.

One of the gringos in there cried, "Jeez!"

Von washed it out with hot water and held it open with two
fingers as he squeezed antiseptic into it. (Such instant medicine was common; once, at the same orphanage, a kid somehow tore a perfect pyramid of meat out of my knuckle. We
had no medicine with us, so we poured perfume into the
hole.) I still had tetanus vaccine in me—the winter before, I
had gotten the two-inch thorn in my foot during the flood at
Las Palmas. The tear in my thigh definitely got my attention.
For the time being, I forgot about the monkey.

If people have it hard on the border, animals have it harder.
Mexicans are often criticized for being cruel. It has caused me
great shame over the years, because it's true. I have seen a
donkey stoned to death by Mexican boys for sport, dogs
poisoned in the Tijuana hills, cats shot. Americans are horrified to find that it is a common practice in Mexico to kick
dogs. I was once shocked out of my wits to find my father
kicking his dog—a dog he loved—savagely. (Yet he was, and
many Mexicans are, extremely softhearted about animals. He
loved cats, which was a rarity in Mexico. He loved birds. In
fact, when he was a boy, he had owned a little goat. It fol-

lowed him everywhere; according to relatives, the goat would walk through town with him and wait outside the door for him to come out. Perhaps it comes as no surprise that someone poisoned it.)

At one orphanage, a much-loved dog, Whiskey, took care of the children. He was part border collie, and he herded them, always lying nearby in the dust, watching them play. When I'd camp out on the mountain behind the place, Whiskey wouldn't let me go alone; after the kids were in bed, he'd find me and sit at the foot of my bed. Inexplicably, someone caught Whiskey and lynched him, leaving him hanging from a tree branch at the entrance to the orphanage.

It doesn't make sense. Mexico is full of dogs that are loved like sons and brothers, but their lives are often utter hell. Sometimes it's the fault of well-meaning Americans. Church groups will occasionally appear at an orphanage with a dog for the kids. This is usually a dog the gringos don't want, and they figure the orphans always need a pup. But when you're trying to feed thirty or sixty kids, spending money on a dog is insanity. Orphanage dogs learn to live on scraps, bread, rotten fruit, bones. If there is a dead animal nearby, they will eat it. Some groups of good conscience think to provide the orphanages with dog food. Certainly if an American gives a dog to an orphanage, it is his duty to keep the dog fed; the dog's suffering, the strain on the orphanage, and the heartbreak for the children are on his head if he doesn't.

We were astounded to find a huge, gorgeous St. Bernard at one orphanage. Everyone was delighted with this dog; a California church had sent him down. He taught me a terrible lesson about food. There was no way that dog could eat enough. No way. They tried to feed him, too. But a 150-pound dog eats a ridiculous amount. Over the weeks I noticed him getting slower and slower, ragged and dull-coated. I didn't think much about him; we were there to work, and we didn't often dawdle. Near the end, I realized that there wasn't any dog left under the hair. Soon he died, slowly starved to death.

Often animals suffer because their masters suffer. Capi was a good example of this. He was a rangy young German shepherd, exceptionally bright and well mannered. He was curious, always poking around, investigating. He was also playful, ready to romp at all hours. Unfortunately, he lived at a fairly poor place, and he had no toys. There were no balls to waste on a dog, for example. No Frisbees.

Capi devised a game with which to keep himself entertained. He discovered that if he picked up a rock and flung it with his head, it would bounce across the yard. He would then chase the rock, catch it, growl at it, shake it, and throw it again. Capi had taught himself to fetch. Late at night, when all the boys were asleep, Capi could be found outside, chasing his rock. One night, though, he picked a rock that was too small. He swallowed it and choked to death in the dark.

As usual, Mexico offers continual bafflement: a middle-class woman I know who didn't like a neighbor's cat's meowing poisoned it; Juanita, in the garbage dump, cuts some of her own food to feed the dump puppies. And the worst animal atrocity I ever saw was perpetrated by a gringo grandpa, and it so outraged a Mexican farmer who was used to butchering hogs and drowning unwanted kittens that he couldn't even come out of his house for fear he would do violence.

A sweet-faced old American man had come to the orphanage with a goat in his trunk. The goat was to be a barbecue for the kids. A *barbacoa* was not uncommon—the goat is butchered and roasted on a bed of hot coals in a pit; the meat comes out tender and succulent, and you eat it with tortillas and beans.

The little goat was nervous, tied to a fence post. I went over and petted it. The kids were milling around, obviously fascinated that the animal was about to be killed.

"You should get the little girls away from here," the grandpa said, " 'cause what we're 'bout to do to this goat isn't too pretty."

He led the goat up the hill with a rope knotted around its neck.

"What we're going to do here is called cold-dressing the meat. Makes it taste less goaty."

A plank was bridged between two greasy oil drums. He picked up the goat and stretched it, kicking, over the plank.

"Done this all the time back at the farm, Dad 'n' me," he said.

The knife was rusty and as dark as blood.

"Let's begin."

He cut a rough hole in the animal's side. The boys, gathered in a circle, tittered in fear as it screamed, little ape-laughs of terror. The old man cut through its two back legs, took a length of rope, and ran it all the way through the holes, jute burning steam from the muscles. The goat shrieked.

The old man threw the end of the rope over a crossbeam above the drum and hauled on it. The little goat jerked up, head down, and swung, a pendulum counting out vast seconds of pain. Hat tipped back, the old man whistled.

You like to think you'll do something at moments like that. If anyone had told me I'd be seeing this scene, I would have told them the old man would be picking up his teeth off the ground. But it doesn't work that way. All I did was stand there, mouth open, shoulders hunched up near my ears.

There was a spigot near us. Attached to it, a long green

hose with the end cut off. Grandpa jammed the rubber into the hole in the goat's side. He worked the hose in deep. Then he walked over to the spigot and turned it on.

Water roared out of the well to the guts, full flood, bloating the entire body. During all this, the goat continued to scream. In mid-bleat, the old man took the knife and cut its throat, brown red and pink spattering his feet. The goat, still struggling, began blowing dark brown bubbles out of its nose like blind eyes, still screaming, though now choking on its own blood. Fans of water squirted through the gash in its throat.

Grandpa said, "We used to fill 'em with ice, back when I was a kid. But, well, no ice around here!"

The goat's cries fell to gurgles, and the man took the knife and pried open the heart. The pendulum circled and slowed, became still. All you could hear was the dripping.

Two weeks after my encounter with the bald monkey, we pulled back into the same orphanage. I had my knee in a tight Ace bandage. There was gauze taped around my thigh. After we ate lunch, I asked the boys how the monkey was. What monkey? they asked. The bald monkey, on the roof. We don't know about any monkey, they said.

I let it go right away. Sometimes you just learn to shrug and forget. Sometimes it's best. Sometimes you just have to focus on what's in front of you, freeze out the rest—he called it cold-dressing, the old grandfather. If you want to sleep, if you want to laugh, if you want to go to church again and believe, ironically, you have to cold-dress your heart. Then press on.

The Stupidity of Evil: Adventures in the Woman Trade

I just ran two illegal aliens across the Arizona desert in my Jeep. The Border Patrol had set up blockades on 19, between Tucson and Nogales. The two women sat in the backseat and blinked at the big Dodge trucks like baby birds. This landscape was harsher than what they were used to—the borderlands around home look down, after all, on Pacific waters. I wondered what the agents would make of my passengers and me if they pulled us over. One of them on an overpass watched me speed by. I wondered about the laws covering human-smuggling; I was counting on the fact that it is one of the few directionally oriented laws in the United States. Law by compass. For, though I was knowingly transporting law-breaking Mexicans, I was heading south. I was smuggling them back into Mexico, so they could get back to Baja, where people are safer on the streets than here.

This is the story of Carmela and Mariposa, a secretary and her next-door neighbor, who have spent their whole lives on our border and never dreamed of coming to the United States. Carmela hadn't been across the border for over twenty years. Mariposa had never been here. The Mexican economy, however, encouraged them.

Carmela's monthly salary was one hundred pesos less than her monthly bills, and her husband's day-labor job was barely making up the difference. They had three kids, one of whom was attending university. His tuition was seven thousand pesos a semester; Carmela and her husband earned six thousand.

One day, a goat rancher named Don Chuy came into Carmela's office. This is where, unexpectedly, I enter as well.

Carmela had known my family when she was younger—she had been, in fact, a close friend to some of my cousins. Don Chuy, in his many journeys into Arizona, had somehow stumbled across a member of the extended family. You know how conversations can go over a few beers. Somehow, the connection was made, and Chuy and his associates hatched their plan after the get-together was over.

He told Carmela that he saw her suffering, trying to make ends meet. He also felt he owed her a favor, since she had looked out for him in a business deal. She was in luck. Did she remember the Urrea family? *Of course*, she said. Well, Don Chuy had an exclusive contract with the Urrea family. They owned factories in the United States, factories so large that they hired busloads of Mexicans to work there. And since she was a family friend, he could guarantee her a good job within a week. Of course, there would be a small fee to get her safely across the border. But it would be much less than what the other coyotes charged.

The Urrea family owns no factories in Tucson.

Carmela's husband was against the idea. He hated the thought of her going away, and he hated the thought of her crossing the dangerous border. "I have a passport," she told him. "I can just walk across the line with the tourists." But, he insisted, even if it was good old Don Chuy, how could he let her travel with a man?

Carmela had an idea: she'd invite Mariposa. Mariposa could be her chaperon, and between Mariposa and Don Chuy, Carmela was sure she'd be safe. They could travel, live, and work together. They'd come home together. And they'd have double the money.

Against his better judgment, Carmela's husband said yes.

Don Chuy had a fit when Carmela showed up at the bus station before dawn accompanied by Mariposa.

"What is this!" he shouted. "I didn't count on this!"

"She'll pay you," Carmela said. "You'll make twice the money."

"This," he sputtered, "is not in the plan! It's dangerous. Very dangerous!"

He immediately donned a pair of sunglasses.

"Act like you don't know me," he said. "Buy your tickets, and get in the back of the bus. Say nothing to anyone!"

He scuttled away, casting suspicious glances in all directions.

They did as they were told. They boarded the bus and took a seat together near the back. They rolled out of town, heading east. It was a long journey ahead of them: Tecate, La Rumorosa, Mexicali, San Luis, Agua Prieta. Don Chuy had snuck into a seat in the front of the bus, never removing his sunglasses. He held a newspaper before his face after the sun came up, pretending to read. When he came back to use the head, he looked away from them, but gestured at them with one hand—some sort of top-secret hand signal.

"This seemed really strange to me," Carmela said later. "We were still in Mexico! We were just taking a bus from one Mexican town to another. Nobody had done anything even slightly illegal."

Carmela was thinking, at this point: *está loco.*

□ □ □ □

When they finally arrived at the Nogales bus station, Don Chuy stood near them and spoke out of the side of his mouth. "Meet me in town," he said. "I'll be in the little square, sitting on a bench under the trees. Watch out for cops. Don't talk to me! Just sit near me and look at a magazine." He hurried out.

The women collected their suitcases and somehow made their way into Nogales.

They found him nervously hiding behind his newspaper. He peered over the edge, eyes still hidden behind his shades, and he nodded once at them. "Sit!" he hissed.

They did.

Everybody sat there.

Suddenly, Don Chuy leaped up and said, "I'll case the park, make sure all's clear. I'll call my contacts."

He moved away and began a circuit of the area. Carmela watched him. He never went near a phone.

In a few minutes, he plopped down and proclaimed: "They're waiting for us. Let's go!"

Later, Carmela admitted, "I should have gone home right then and there."

They followed Don Chuy to meet his smuggling contacts.

Carmela was right. All she had to do was walk through the checkpoint. Don Chuy was five people ahead of her, looking over his shoulder and smiling too much. "Vacation," Carmela said to the bored gringo checking everybody's papers. They were through.

They convened in the tiny park in Nogales, U.S.A., near the gazebo. Behind them, the train tracks. All around them, the old men who call themselves the "CPW" (City Park Winos). Don Chuy, behind his shaking newspaper, looked just like one of them. Perhaps that was his plan all along—foil the Border Patrol by blending in with the garrulous bums of Nogales. If he'd been nervous before, he was positively jumping out of his skin now.

"Don't look at me!" he said. "Don't talk to me!" Carmela thought he was having a stroke. His face, as they waited for Mariposa, began to turn purple.

Mariposa was in the hands of Don Chuy's "associates." They had turned out to be a bunch of young thugs who took her money and made her carry her own suitcase. They added her to a small group of females—a pregnant woman and a gaggle of teens who were on their way to Phoenix to be maids. "Let's go," the head smuggler said.

"But we don't know where we're going," Mariposa said.

"So?" He shrugged. "Head out, we'll follow you."

Off they went, a thoroughly lost Mariposa leading the way.

The thugs sauntered along behind them, doing a version of Don Chuy's undercover routine. When it came time to direct the women to turn, the smugglers would cough and clear their throats and bark out a word. Mariposa was not always sure she'd heard right. *"Cough.* Left! *Ahem! Cough-cough!* Right!"

They turned right.

"Here we are," the smugglers said. "Good luck."

They hurried away with the women's money.

The women looked at each other. The smugglers had delivered them into the traffic lane driving through the border gate. Drivers goggled up at them as they stood there. All they had to do was run down the line of cars, get by the Border Patrol, and they'd be in the U.S.A.

"I want my money back," Mariposa said.

□ □ □ □

The teenaged girls ran. They charged through the gate before the INS officer knew what hit him. He stepped out of his booth and yelled, "Hey!"

The pregnant woman built up a head of steam and charged. The guard jumped out and reached for her but she slipped past. "Hey, goddamnit!" he hollered.

Mariposa took hold of her suitcase with two hands and started to jog.

He hung his head out and glared at her.

"Ay," she said, and turned away to skulk behind some trucks.

When he wasn't looking, she charged out and galloped toward the gate. He stepped out and waggled a finger at her. Mariposa, trying to look like she jogged through United States–bound traffic carrying heavy luggage every day, turned away and trotted along, gazing at the fence.

The third time, she almost made it, but he leaped out and snagged the collar of her coat. She must have seemed like one of those Warner Bros. cartoon dogs who speed to the ends of their leashes and *Boiiing!* suddenly fly backward. He towered over her, and he was plenty mad. He bellowed in her face; she understood nothing: "Habba-dabba-babba-rabba!" he was yelling. There was only one word she clearly heard. And that was: *arrested.* She hung her head and trudged back into Mexico. The road signs above her head all said: MEXICO, NO EXIT.

"I'm going back for her," Carmela said.

"No!" Don Chuy was shouting. "No! I never counted on this! Leave her!"

"I won't."

Carmela put her bags beside Don Chuy and started walking. He hid behind the newspaper and trembled.

Mariposa was discovered leaning on the fence and gazing morosely into Arizona. Carmela crossed over and said, "Just follow me. We'll bluff our way through the checkpoint."

They got in line.

Carmela was hoping the gringo checking the papers had been so bored that he'd not noticed her the first time she went through. Then, she would try to get her passport into Mariposa's hand. Mariposa didn't look anything like Carmela's picture, but if the gringo was *that* bored, it might work.

If front of them, a group of Americanos was trying to carry several wicker chairs through. There was some kind of bottleneck, and the lone *migra* officer turned away for a moment and started looking for something. "Go!" Carmela said and walked by, waving her passport. Mariposa hurried after her, waving something over her head—it was probably her social-security ID, and they were out the door and bearing down on Don Chuy before the *migra* officer even noticed.

A second top-secret bus trip, this time heading north. Same routine. Don Chuy, about to have some sort of coronary event, sat at the front. They watched his ears turn purple.

When they got into Tucson, he motioned for them to stand outside in the parking lot. They pondered the Hotel Congress while he used the pay phone.

"We're in," he said, when he joined them. "Our contact will be here in a few minutes to collect you."

"What about the Urreas?" Carmela asked.

"The Urreas?" he said, suddenly cagey. "Oh, you know. They're busy. As soon as the coast is clear, we'll call them. It's a big business. We can't bring heat down on them."

A large truck arrived. The doors swung open. The driver was named Fidel. He continues to work in transportation in Pima county. He wore a uniform.

"Let's go," he said.

He drove them in circles. Carmela, already disoriented, was completely lost. By the time the sun was setting, she could only see that they were driving into "the worst part of Tucson." She was nervous.

Fidel pulled up to a stucco one-story house.

"My wife left me," he said. "I'm all alone in my house. I need a woman's touch."

This struck both women as an odd confession, but it was only in keeping with all the other weird events of the day.

"Boy," Mariposa said to Carmela, "illegal-alien smuggling is a strange business."

They thought Don Chuy was going to stay and protect them.

"I have to get back to the ranch!" he announced. Downland from the border, his ranch was somewhere east of Ensenada. "I have a sick goat!"

A sick goat? Carmela thought. *How does he know a goat is sick?*

Don Chuy hurried away, and Fidel locked the door.

"I don't have a bed for you," he said. "You'll have to sleep on the floor in the laundry room. Take the pillows off the couch. Sorry, but my wife took all the blankets."

He was eyeing Carmela.

"She didn't like to have sex. I needed sex all the time."

With this interesting tidbit, he went to the living room to have a drink.

Mariposa vowed to stay awake all night, guarding Carmela.

"He was a pervert," she said later. "I could tell right away. What kind of man makes ladies sleep on the floor and tells them terrible things about sex?"

Again, Fidel mentioned his aching sexual needs to the women.

Carmela spoke up: "What about the Urreas?" she said. "We're here to speak to the Urreas."

He sneered.

"You must take us to the Urreas!" she insisted.

He went away and came back with a phone book. He threw it on the floor.

"Look them up," he said. "Maybe we'll try to find them tomorrow."

The women cuddled on the cement floor on couch pillows, with their coats and two other pillows covering them.

Mariposa started to cry.

"Something's wrong," she said.

In the morning, Fidel had no breakfast for them. He handed them brooms. "Clean up the place," he ordered them. "You don't expect to stay here for free?" He stared at Carmela. "We'll talk about rent later."

He went to his den and started calling people on the telephone. He was speaking in English, so they couldn't understand what he was saying. Carmela said, "Don't worry," and went outside to sweep off his porch. Mariposa snuck to the hall cabinets and opened the doors. The shelves were crammed full of blankets and comforters.

She heard Fidel laugh.

She snuck to the door of his den and heard him say, in Spanish, "I have a special shipment in. Yeah, they're here now. Fresh. Two new ones. Going cheap, too."

She hurried out to Carmela.

All they could think to do was to insist that the Urrea family be contacted. Carmela raised such a ruckus that Fidel finally said, "All right!"

He took them to his truck and drove around Tucson again.

After driving them up and down Campbell, back and forth on Broadway, then down to Ajo and Valencia, he pulled into a Circle K on Twenty-second. "Couldn't find the factory," he said. "What should I do now?" He smiled at them.

Carmela startled him by jumping out of the truck.

She had looked up phone numbers in the directory when he'd thrown it on the floor.

"What are you doing?" he yelled.

"I'll call!" she said. "Don't worry! Come on, Mariposa!"

Mariposa made a face at Fidel and hopped out. Carmela was already at the pay phone, scrambling to get a quarter in the slot. Fidel started to step out of the truck. Carmela called a number and accidentally caught an Urrea who spoke Spanish and who knew the woman she was trying to reach.

"Help me, please," Carmela said.

She smiled happily and waved at Fidel.

Furious, he slammed his door and sped out of the lot, rocketing over dips in the alley. Before he could circle back on them, they were hiding down the street, watching for the Urrea Cavalry to come.

We stood at the doorway of the bus station in Nogales. They were back, only days after their pointless journey had begun. Don Chuy had taken a hundred dollars from each of them—for nothing. Fidel had charged them a fee to help them get settled in their new factory jobs. The thugs at the border had charged Mariposa for the opportunity to run for her life. And, somewhere in Tucson, there was a room prepared for them, a place where "fresh shipments" of women were apparently delivered.

Carmela was crying. She said, "Don Chuy never expected me to come home."

"No," I said.

"But he knew they would hurt us," she said.

"Or kill us," said Mariposa.

"That's why he was so scared."

"He was already breaking the law when you got on the bus," I said. "He was kidnapping you."

"Ay Dios!"

We hugged each other. They were going home with less than they had started out with. But they were alive. There was that.

"My husband . . . ," Carmela said. "You don't know what he's like. He . . . he will kill Don Chuy."

I have to admit, it didn't knock me to my knees in horror.

"Perhaps," I suggested, "Don Chuy should have taken that into consideration."

Mariposa crinkled up her nose in disgust.

"If you steal women," she said to me, "I think getting killed by their husbands is one of the risks of your career. If he doesn't kill that old man, I might!"

"Turn him over to the cops," I said.

"Let them kill him," Mariposa said.

"You're not too worried about Don Chuy," Carmela said.

Mariposa picked up her suitcase and looked out at Nogales one last time. "He should have stuck to his goats."

They pushed inside just in time to catch the last bus home.

A Day in the Life

Work is a vow that heaven never ignores.
—JUSTO SEIRRA

Five A.M., and the sounds of sleeping still fill the house. Doña Juana rises first, climbing from the slumping bed as Don Manuel still snores lightly, the swollen knuckles on his left hand glistening in the dull light as blood seeps from the cracks in his leathery skin. He, like everyone else, calls her Juanita, little Juana, which has nothing to do with size and everything to do with affection. You could say it means "my little Juana."

Doña Juana sleeps in her clothes—this morning, she wears baggy Levi's provided by a gringo missionary group, new underpants worn for only two days, and a Metallica T-shirt. Although she can smell Don Manuel and the mists rising from the children and the other sleepers, she can no longer smell herself. Her breasts swing loosely under the T-shirt, long now, and nursed to the point of collapse. Her hair is turning white—lightning bolts seem to cut through her dense rope of hair, swirling down the double braid in pale corkscrews. She is missing seven teeth, and the sight of her own naked flesh alarms her. She is covered in stretch marks, scars, bites, varicose veins, and pouches of collapsed skin. She is four feet nine inches tall. She is forty-two years old.

She pulls on a battered pair of Keds dock shoes and pads

out of the bedroom on her new cement floor. Manuel saved up and bought two sacks of cement. He and the neighbors made a party out of it, mixing and pouring the floor. One corner sags, but the rest of it is pretty flat. She must have one of the girls sweep: orange peels, paper, dirt, collect in the corners. She shakes her head—it's impossible to keep house. She has two rooms and a kitchen to take care of. It's too much.

She pulls aside the blanket that serves as a door as she passes into the front room. The bedroom wall wobbles as she walks through the doorway. Manuel and the boys hammered it together out of scrap wood, paper, cardboard boxes, and some water-warped *rocanrol* posters. Small pictures of Jesus, saints, and the Virgin of Guadalupe adorn the wall and cover holes. The only other decoration, in a cheap wooden frame bought in the Woolworth's downtown (they pronounce it *Goolgoort's*), is Manuel's certificate of military service. He graduated from the army a full private, and its multicolored filigree looks important to the family. It is important: an accomplishment recognized by the government. Written on the wall in Magic Marker, three inches to the right, is *"Viva Colosio, Salvador de la Gente."* This was written by Lalo, the neighbor, because neither Manuel nor Juanita knows how to write. But since Colosio was assassinated on a campaign stop downtown, he has become a beloved figure of liberation to them all. As of yet there are no plaster Colosio busts, only increasingly rare PRI-party presidential campaign posters with Russian Revolution–style portraits of the candidate staring off in the distance. The best they can do is graffiti.

They all gathered at Lalo's house to watch the assassination on Lalo's television. The gun was clear in the picture, floating out of the crowd, Lalo said, just like a bird. And they saw it: it did float out, sudden yet slow, deadly blunt, and so matter-of-fact that it looked fake. *Pop.* Colosio's hair mussed as if by a stiff breeze, and he fell, and their hopes toppled with him.

Lalo found his TV in the dump, and the knobs were gone, so he took knobs off another TV. The power came from a bank of salvaged car batteries and intricate wiring that only Lalo knew to connect. Manuel has been calling him the Spider because of his mad electrical webbing. But the night of the assassination, there were no jokes. Juanita wept. Nobody could understand this new thing: they have killed tomorrow in Tijuana.

"It reminds me," Manuel said, "of when the gringos killed Kennedy."

"Who?" Lalo asked.

Behind Juanita, in stacked bunk beds and on a mattress on the floor, separated from Manuel by a hanging sheet, thirteen people sleep in a room twelve feet by ten feet. Of these thirteen, seven are her own children; one daughter among them, little Perla, is seven months pregnant. One person, Don Manuel, is her husband. Two are grandchildren. One is the boyfriend of her eldest daughter, and the last two are cousins recently arrived from the garbage dump in Mexico City.

The power struggle in the Mexico City dump has driven them north, to Tijuana. The warring mafias that control the trash are locked in a subterranean *Godfather* scenario. The ancient don who ruled the trash and the trash-pickers has died, and his progeny have divided into factions, each of them battling to be King of the Trash. Gunmen and goon squads are recruiting supporters, and in its own small way, the Mexico City dump has become as complex and dangerous as the old Revolution. Trash-pickers have also had to become political analysts to survive. Like many tiny Latin American nations, the Mexico City dump has become too harsh for its citizens—they're heading north.

The young couple, sleeping together in a bottom bunk, move together under the blankets and slyly make love, rocking gently so as not to wake the others. One of the cousins, however, lies quietly in his bed and watches the woman's face as the blanket pulls away, watches her eyes roll up, close. Then a smile crosses her lips. She opens her eyes and looks right at him. He blushes, ducks his head. He hears her gasp. He thinks of home.

His name is Braulio.

The missionaries have given Doña Juana a small Coleman two-burner stove. Manuel has converted the white gas tank into a small propane system. Every week Manuel has the tank recharged downtown, at the propane tank yards. Tijuana does not have a gas system like San Diego's. Each house has a silver or white tank outside, and anyone who has grown up in Tijuana is used to the hollow ring of the tanks being loaded on and off trucks. Gas, like potable water, is delivered by ugly trucks from the 1950s and early 1960s. On delivery day, the rusty *cloing* can be heard up and down the street. It's a homey sound, as sentimental as a gringo's memory of tinkling milk bottles on the porch—Mexican sounds, like the sound of the ice cream man's bell as he pushes his little two-wheeled cart along the street, the mailman's harsh whistle that sounds almost like a toy train. Doña Juana, of course, knows none of these sounds.

She turns the key and is amazed, afraid a little—as if this were some sorcery, and it probably is, because who has ever heard of such a thing. She ponders the ice that forms along the gas feed line. Wads of frost make a snowball where the line joins the burners. "Leave it to gringos," she will say, "to make ice from fire."

There is no sink. Manuel built her a counter out of a plank of plywood. Later he cut a hole in it and put a plastic tub down the hole, to hold the plates. Manuel, she thinks, is a genius. He can build anything. And the counter is covered with filthy plates, plates caked and clotted with grease and old food. Flies already work the corners of the kitchen—her one frying pan still has a fistful of fried rice and tomato in it, and it has dried a sickly orange, and the flies walk over it, prod their suckers into it, and settle their rear ends deep among the hard kernels. She waves at them abstractedly, takes the pan to the front door, and dumps the rice on the dusty ground. There her piglet and a small dog fight for a bite.

No water. She hasn't bathed in a week, and there has been no water to wash things for . . . she can't remember. Their one water bottle, a five-gallon glass jug mounted on a metal frame, is half empty. She grabs the neck of the jug, tips it, and pours cloudy water into the coffeepot.

The smell of coffee, she knows, will awaken Manuel.

And their day can begin.

Five-thirty A.M.

Don Manuel rises slowly, puts his feet on the paper-thin green carpet beside the bed, and rests his head in his hands. He has a hangover, but it's not from drinking. He doesn't know what has gotten into his head, but in the mornings there is a nauseating ache behind his forehead. It feels green to him somehow. His ears hum and his joints ache. But he won't say anything. They can't afford the doctor, and it embarrasses him to go to the missionaries. And besides, doctors are for children and women.

He sits and thinks over his list of chores for the day. Is

there anything he missed yesterday? For a moment, he feels a bolt of panic—did he remember to get new rags for Juanita? It is her month again, and he promised to get her some clean cloths to make the pad. He feels a surge of adrenaline inside his body—this too is new, this sense of panic. Juanita and her blood, spilling out of her like life itself. Most couples don't talk of these things, but his old woman and he like to talk. Maybe that's what gives him the hangovers—staying up too late, whispering. There was a time, sure, when he went astray. He had sex with six women in the neighborhood, and he knows that black Cuquis bore him a son. But suddenly, and he can't explain it, Juanita became dear to him again. She was cutting the head off a chicken, and he immediately realized he loved her. She seemed so small to him then, so brave in the morning sun. The blood flew all over her arms, glistening like jewels. Though he has no word for *glisten*, he can imagine what jewels in the sun would look like. Like sparkling red water.

His *compadre* Lalo, two shacks down, says Juanita put a love hex on Manuel. "Nobody falls back in love with their wives," he tells Manuel. "Not after all the women we have had. She gave you the *agua de coco*." Manuel shudders—*agua de coco* (coconut water), a brew of menses mixed in with the coffee. Which brings him back to Juana's period, and he remembers that he collected several lengths of white terrycloth at the recycling center, and she carefully folded them into pads right here on the bed. "I will be dry soon," she told him. "No more blood. No more rags. I'm an old woman."

"No more sons?" he said.

She shook her head.

Thank God, she was thinking, but she didn't tell him that.

When they had paper towels and napkins, they were the best lining to put inside the cloth pads. They could be thrown away, and the pads could last twice as long. But this month there are no napkins.

Some gringa missionaries brought down things the women stick inside themselves, but who ever heard of such a thing? They must have been Protestants. It was an insult, and probably some kind of sin. Manuel didn't know about these *cristianos* sometimes. The women had burned the terrible little objects in shame after the missionaries were gone. They wouldn't even let the children use the plastic parts for toys.

Oh, well.

Manuel stretches, winces, and rises.

Braulio, the cousin from Mexico City, silently rises behind Manuel. He loves the morning, when he can think for a minute. He says his prayers, not only to Jesus and la Virgen but to the saint of his almost forgotten village in Michoacán. He can't remember the saint's name, but he can remember her face, carved in wood, her slight smile, her flaking, blue-painted eyes. Braulio sits in the dull light and watches the faces of the children as they start to stir. Like the morning, the children are something he loves. He dreams of a family of his own. His fantasies include detailed plans for a new tar-paper shack. Something beautiful, something sophisticated, with a covered walkway to the outhouse and actual glass in the windows. He has figured that a central open space can be used for fires, and those fires can not only light the main room but warm the house. He can't quite figure out how to get the smoke out without leaving an opening in the roof for rain to come in. He sees the fire in his mind. The dirt floor. The small pen in the kitchen for the ducks and chickens. It is a perfect house. When he has paper, he sketches it, placing the imaginary furniture and children in the paper rooms.

Braulio touches the face of the little girl awakening beside him. She snuffles and grimaces and slaps at his hand, rolls over. He smiles. He turns and looks across the room. He is in love with little pregnant Perla. The Pearl. The father of the baby went across the border. Perla has been waiting for him to come back, but it's obvious to everyone, even her, that he won't return. Braulio doesn't mind that she's pregnant. It's that much more work already done. She already contains his family, if she'll have him. One day he's going to have to tell her. But he gets nervous. Love does that to a man. Besides, the thought of tasting her milk arouses him, and he's sure she can sense his deviant thoughts, and it makes him feel shame. He prays to the saint to remove these desires from his heart. And he looks at Perla's smoky face and her stiff explosion of black hair on the coat she uses for a pillow, and he sighs.

Was there ever a more beautiful girl?

Six A.M.

"Do we have anything to eat, *vieja?*" Manuel asks.

"No, *viejo.*"

She pours him a cup of black coffee.

"Doughnuts?"

She pulls back her hair.

"Manuel," she says, "you know those were for the children."

"And who has to work like a mule all day?" he snaps. "The children or me?" He sips his coffee. "Besides," he says, "today is bath day. They'll get more *donas.*"

She sucks at her teeth for a moment, then says, "You're right." Today the missionaries are coming. She has a crush on the pastor, *el famoso hermano*, but he doesn't even know she exists. Still, she'd like to be home, just to see him. A little flirting never hurt anybody. It doesn't mean she doesn't love her Manuelito. She looks at him, his skinny neck and his huge black mustache. He has gold trim on his teeth. My man, she thinks. But she doesn't forget her pastor, either.

She puts two stiff glazed doughnuts on the table. The missionaries collected them from a Winchell's in San Diego, and they have lain frozen in a gringo garage for a month.

"I'll get some beans too," she says. "Maybe some potatoes."

He offers her a piece of doughnut. She shakes her head.

"It's all right, *viejo*. I'm on a diet."

"Hm," he grunts. He goes to the door with his cup. "Another hot day," he says, then steps outside. He sticks his head back in the door and says, "See if the missionaries have any applesauce."

"*Ay, Dios*," she replies. "We all know you can't live without your applesauce!"

"Every parrot to his perch," he says.

They laugh.

It makes him cough.

He turns back out the door and spits—the tiny dog at his feet barely skips away before he's hit.

Six-fifteen A.M.

He sees his *compadre*, Lalo, standing out in the street.

"*Oye, tú, pinche buey*," he says.

"*Vete a la chingada, pinche puto cabrón*," Lalo says.

Insults taken care of, they wave and grin.

"What time are you going to work?" Manuel says.

"Now, brother."

"Well, fuck."

"No other way." Lalo shrugs.

"That's life," Manuel agrees.

"That's life."

"Life."

"Fucking life!"

"There," Manuel says, taking one last gulp of coffee, "you have said it all, *compa*. You don't have to say another word, because you have said it all right there."

He steps back inside to pull on his work shoes and collect his tools.

Manuel says to Juanita, "Lalo said *pinche* life."

"Ay, Lalo," she says.

These are Manuel's work tools:

One pair of battered leather gloves, which he carries tucked into the back pocket of his pants; the way these gloves hang out and dangle is part of garbage-dump fashion. A snappy dresser will have the gloves so worn down that they're soft, and the fingers should fall flat against the man's buttocks. Although canvas gloves drape better, leather gloves are preferred.

A baseball cap to keep the sun out of his eyes.

A second pair of pants—loose and dirty dress slacks one size too big. These go on over Manuel's Levi's, as a kind of protective skin. They will catch the majority of the dump's filth and can be peeled off at the end of the day. When there's water, Juanita can boil them in a tin tub over a fire. If they get too contaminated, Manuel might drop them right there, in the trash. Often someone else will come along and pick them up: there are distinct classes among the trash-pickers, and some trash-pickers pick the castoffs of others.

Along with the second pair of pants, a shirt put on over a relatively clean T-shirt. The same rules apply: the shirt is his second skin.

A bandana for the sweat, and to be worn over the face as an occasional gas mask.

Work shoes.

Bags: bags are very valuable. Bags are Manuel's briefcase and his wheelbarrow. He will often tie a rope around his waist and tuck several plastic bags into the rope. The bags too can be a fashion statement.

The multipurpose pole carried over the shoulder like a cane fishing pole.

If times are good, he might take a little lunch with him, or he might buy a festering torta or taco from a lunch wagon that brings its smoky wares into the dump. Sneaking in behind the long parade of dumptrucks, the lunch wagon pulls off to the side and opens for business. Although relatively far away from the actual garbage, the food is touched by flies and smoke and dust clouds coming out of the trash.

And these are Juanita's work tools, for she works alongside her man, everyone equal in the garbage:

One clear plastic produce bag, tucked into her underwear and placed between the pads and her clothes.

Otherwise, she is dressed almost exactly like her husband. Except she tucks her canvas gloves into the front of her pants. And she's worried about her shoes.

"I like these shoes, *viejo*," she says. "I hate to ruin them."

"Put bags on them," he says.

"*Estás loco*. I'll look like a fool with my feet in bags."

"That's true," he says, buttoning his pants. "You always like to look nice." He combs his hair. "I have an idea."

"What."

"Put white bags over your shoes. That will look really good."

She smiles.

"Yes," she says. "That's good. *Es muy sexy*."

"Wow!" he says, which is his favorite word in English.

□ □ □ □

Six-thirty A.M.

Braulio steps into the kitchen and says, *"Buenos días."*

"Buenos días," Manuel and Juanita say in unison.

Braulio dips his head at them, almost a bow. He still feels like an interloper, though they have made him feel at home.

"I know where I can get some eggs," he says.

"Eggs!" cries Manuel. "Who can afford eggs!"

"No money, *m'ijo,*" Juanita says.

Braulio shows them some coins that he has been storing in his pocket. They lean in and look. Manuel's eyebrows rise.

"Three gringo quarters," Braulio says, using the Spanglish word: *quattahs.* "I was going to buy a beer," he says. "But let's have eggs."

"Wow," Manuel repeats. "Wow. Yeah-yeah." He's a hipster. Braulio can't imagine being as cool as Manuel. "Shit!"

"Shat," Braulio says.

"No, shit."

"Shet."

"No seas pendejo, socio. Shit."

"Chit!"

Braulio rushes out to buy a few eggs from one of the neighbors.

"He's a good boy," Juanita says.

"He's bit of a *pendejo,*" says Manuel, putting on his cap. "But he's all right."

Juanita sticks her head into the bedroom and shrieks, "Get up!"

Six forty-five A.M.

One of the little sisters sits on the floor in a stupor. She can never quite wake up with everyone else. She is still possessed by her dreams, and is sometimes so lost in the fog that she urinates in her pants before she manages to get up and go to the hole. She often smells of pee. Manuel calls her *huevona*, which loosely translated means "girl with big balls," which somehow means "lazy." Braulio picks her up and says, "Let's have *huevos, huevona*," which makes her giggle. *Huevos* being eggs as well as balls. So maybe Manuel is saying she's a brood hen, sitting on eggs instead of working.

The lovers have already risen from their bunk bed and made their way out the door. They won't be seen again till evening. Off sniffing glue and smoking *mota* with the other pot-heads. Braulio doesn't know where they get money for the marijuana, though rumor has it that she lets the junkies touch her breasts for trade. Juanita and Manuel have spoken often of throwing the couple out, but they don't want to betray family.

Braulio and Perla are left in charge of the children.

Everyone else, aside from the pot-heads, is outside, getting ready for work.

Seven-fifteen A.M.

Lalo is parked outside in his pickup, angry again. He's mad every morning. "Hurry up, *cabrones!*" he shouts. Every day he wants to leave for work by seven, and every day everybody meanders around and makes him late. He would go without them, but they each pay him a few cents for rides to and from work. "The worst part about us Mexicans," he turns and tells Manuel—who is always on time—"is that we're always late."

"With any luck," Manuel replies, "we'll be late for our graves."

Lalo lights a cigarette and says, "You call that luck?"

Juanita doesn't want to ride in the cab. She prefers the bed, jammed in comfortably with eight other trash-pickers, where she can feel the wind, smell the clean scent of the ocean as they drive, see the bright colors of the *segunda*, the big outdoor flea market she usually can't afford to visit. Juanita loves to see the Pacific, sparkling and so blue, just beyond the hills. And the islands out there, right off the coast, looking so close she dreams she can swim to them. Little paradises right by the *dompe*. And the white flecks of San Diego shine on good days too, like small frozen waves on the beach.

Marilu is having trouble getting on. Juanita reaches down to her and says, "We're getting old, Mari."

"Speak for yourself," Mari says. "I'm just fat!"

They all laugh.

Lalo puts it in gear and does his best to ease over the big rocks in the road.

Seven twenty-five A.M.

Lalo has stopped again, cursing and shaking the wheel. He has hit a rock and thrown Hermanita Consuelo face-first against the back window. She is easily seventy years old, though some say she is eighty. She wears girlish makeup and low-cut dresses. Her necklines reveal a chest that looks like parchment stretched over chicken bones. Her shiny bodice often reveals the acornlike stubs of her bosoms. Her lips are always bright crimson, and her cheeks are powdered pale white, and her eyes always bear heavy black pencil lines around them. She has one long orange fang in the front of her mouth. All of her children are dead, and some of the men in the barrio reportedly sneak in to visit her at night, when her husband is asleep. Consuelo still loves la Marilyn Monroe.

She has a bloody nose, and the others in the back have forced Lalo to stop. Hermanita Consuelo is spread out in the bed of the pickup, holding her nose, and all the biddies back there hover over her and cluck.

"Ay," Consuelo moans. "Ay ay."

"Poor little thing," Mari says. "That mule Lalo broke her nose."

Another pickup pulls over and the driver calls out, "Lalo! Who did you kill this time?"

Lalo waves him off.

"A man," he says, "just can't get ahead in this world."

Manuel cranes his head around and stares at the tableau behind them.

"Poor old woman," he says.

"If she doesn't like the service," Lalo grumbles, "let her buy her own truck."

Juanita jumps down.

"I'm going to take the *hermanita* back home, all right?"

Manuel gets out of the cab and looks in at Hermanita Consuelo.

There is a dark red cut across the bridge of her nose. Her eyes are loose in her head. Blood everywhere.

"Is she all right?"

Juanita shrugs.

"She will be, if God wills it. But I'm going to take her home. She can't work like this."

"All right," he says. "Maybe the missionaries can fix her." He puts his hand on Juanita's arm. "You probably should go home anyway. You know." He glances at her belly.

"Will you be all right, *viejo?*"

"Sure. I'll be able to visit all my girlfriends without you there spying on me all day," he jokes.

She cocks an eyebrow at him and pulls away.

"Work hard," she says.

"Like a burro," he replies.

He watches his woman lead the old hag down the road, and it's hard to tell what he's feeling. He's holding up the commute, but he just stands there. Lalo has given up at this point:

all the best spots will already be populated by now, and either he's going to have to sneak around till he finds a gap in the work crews or he'll have to shame himself by asking somebody if he can move in beside them. Oh, well. He was planning to make an extra couple of dollars this week for beer. He watches Manuel watching his fat little Juanita. Lalo shakes his head. It's starting to seem like Manuel thinks they have all day. Like he wants to go home with his wife.

On the radio, they're playing that damned *conjunto punk* from Mexico City, Caifanes. They're singing, "I wish I were alcohol, so I could evaporate within you."

Lalo, watching Manuel in his rearview mirror, thinks about love potions and women's fierce magics. He says, *"Agua de coco."*

Eight-thirty A.M.

Juanita comes home and finds Perla in the kitchen, talking to Cuquis. Juanita suspects Cuquis of messing around with Manuel, but she can't prove it. Cuquis has a certain glamour in the neighborhood—she's from the east coast somewhere and has a strange accent as well as black blood. The only way she could be more exotic is if she had blue eyes and red hair. She and Perla stir as Juanita enters, and Juanita says, "Don't get up."

She tips herself a glass of water.

"The *hermanita* broke her nose."

They all tsk-tsk over the old woman's misfortune.

"No work today," says Cuquis.

"Not for her."

"Not for me," Perla says.

Cuquis stretches, says, "We were talking about being with the big belly." *Panzona.*

Perla is rubbing her abdomen. She says, "Do you know the weirdest thing about being pregnant?"

Cuquis and Juanita, who know all too much about being pregnant, smile.

"No," says Juana. "What, *m'ija?*"

"The weirdest thing about being pregnant is . . . well, there's two things. No, wait—there's *three* weirdest things about being pregnant."

Cuquis snaps, "All right! So what are they!"

Perla sticks her tongue out at Cuquis.

"Con esa lengua," Cuquis says, *"mi perro se lamea el culo."* It is so obscene that all three women burst out laughing, crying *"Ay, Dios"* and *"Ay, Cuca—¡no te aguantas!"*

Cuquis has told them, "With that tongue, my dog licks his asshole."

Juanita turns to heat more coffee.

"Coffee, Cuca?"

"Sí."

Perla still wants to talk about her pregnancy. "First," she says, "it's my belly button. It popped out, like the baby pushed it out."

Juanita says, "He did push it out, *m'ija*. I remember mine poking out. Cuca?"

Cuquis shakes her head.

"I always have a perfect body, even when I'm pregnant."

"Uy-uy," says Juanita. "You think you're so hot."

"I am hot."

Perla cuts them off. "Now it sticks out like a big thumb. My nephew saw me the other day and it was sticking out of my shirt and he said, 'Look at Auntie Perla—she has a *pipí!*' "

The women chuckle. Juanita pours them each a cup of coffee.

"And?" she says.

"The second weirdest thing is when it moves."

Juanita says, "Oh, yes."

"Restless little devils," Cuca notes.

"It kicks my liver like a *futbol!*" cries Perla.

"They do that."

"He wants room service," Cuquis says. "He's calling for a big supper, like the actors do on television."

"*Oye*, Cuca," Juanita says, "where did you ever see television?"

"All my boyfriends," Cuquis boasts, "have televisions."

"What about your husband?"

"That good-for-nothing? No television. Why do you think I have boyfriends!"

"Ay, Cuca!"

"*Cuca, Cuca, eres tremenda!*"

Perla says, "And the third thing . . ." Worried, she looks into her own shirt. "It's my . . . *nipples.* They got so big!"

Juanita and Cuca are smiling.

"Is it normal?" Perla asks in a small voice.

"*Ay, muchacha,*" Cuquis says. "Wait until the milk comes."

"It's all right, Perla," Juanita says. "They get big—"

Cuquis: "Brown like chocolate."

"Mine are already brown, Cuca!" Perla cries.

"Then they'll get as black as old *atole.* They'll look like licorice."

Perla makes a face.

"Really?"

"These things happen, *m'ija,*" Juanita says. "God has His little surprises for women."

"I wish He'd asked me what I thought about it," Perla says.

"Don't blaspheme," Cuquis replies.

□ □ □ □

Ten A.M.

The dump itself is a vast scatter of bright specks. The trash lies across the land in layers of dull colors enlivened by exclamation points of white plastic and paper. From a hillside, it looks like a Pollock canvas in full frenzy. And above, in swirling disks, rise the thousands of gulls. They look as if the white flecks on the ground have become animated and have begun to spiral out of the frame. So many gulls fill the bright sky that the ocean beyond is pale, as if seen through a thin bank of fog. And moving back and forth, slowly, hunched, looking like strange little birds picking insects out of the soil, the humans work. They stay silent because the noise drowns out their words. They blend with the garbage, become invisible for a moment against the camouflage. Then they move back into the sunlight—cranes, ibises, storks—but it takes effort to see them as people. And roving hugely among them, fat and wicked, exploding noxious black clouds of smoke and looking like dragons, dinosaurs, carnivorous giants, come the tractors. Big bulldozers with iron spikes on their treads, and earthmovers pulling their pregnant-looking sleds behind them. Even from a mile away, they can be heard growling, belching, coughing. At times, when the wind is right, their engines sound just like animals. Some meat-eater ripping at a corpse, the gear-shifting making them sound like they're growling. And every few bites, they pause to roar.

Eleven A.M.

The children have been playing in the dirt. Perla is napping. Juanita listlessly sweeps the rooms, thinking of home. She can remember poking ripe mangoes out of the trees with a long stick. Once, as a special treat, her grandmother had fried cow brains and eggs. Once she saw her mother and father making love. Once there was a flood, and they saw a shack go by, complete, as if it had been built on the water, and there were people on the roof, crying out as they were swept into the night. These memories pass slowly through her mind. She never thinks about sex.

Braulio is outside, and he strains against a large broken wooden frame, one of the many bits of scrap and trash littering the yard, and he is thinking about sex. He overheard the women talking about breasts, and it has made him feel frantic. Perla is on his mind. He would like to sneak in the room and lie beside her. He wants to feel the roundness of her belly. He turns his back on the kids shrieking in the dirt and heaves once more against the wood. He has been wondering if he should go to school. He will have to earn money to care for Perla and his—the—baby. He isn't going to stay in the trash. He has that new house to build. He wants to buy a television. And a book. He wants to read. He wipes his brow. He wishes he had a tape recorder or a radio. Music is like reading a book with your ears. He heard a word he liked, and he feels it is true about him. Lalo said it about him, and he thinks it is the highest compliment he has ever received. The word is *filosófico*.

Noon.

Huevona sits on the summit of the hill that separates the neighborhood from the rest of the world. She still smells like pee. She wears her crusty underpants, a green pair of pants under a one-piece dress, a sleeveless undershirt under the dress. Her socks are unmatched, and she wears shoes that were once white. She's watching for the missionary vans. Her smell comforts her, though she is just vaguely aware that it bothers others. They complain about it all the time. She doesn't understand why.

Clouds of dust appear below, moving steadily up the road.

"*¡Los americanos!*" she yells, jumping to her feet and running through the neighborhood. "*¡Los americanos!*" People come out and start to hustle toward the community basketball court, where the vans will park in a semicircle. The women are already carrying their mesh and plastic bags. There are only ten men in the throng, and they are all old, sick, or drunk. All the other men are either in the trash or in San Diego.

Juanita and Perla hurry along, trying to beat the sharks. These sharks are outsiders, women who come from miles away, walking hours to get some of the American goods. There are often fistfights between locals and sharks, the women rolling around on the ground in deadly clutches, choking and punching as they roll, while their friends and neighbors laugh and taunt them and occasionally kick them.

The bathing rooms are already waiting. The gringos pay a small rent to two families for the use of their buildings. One of them, Hermana Josefina, is a Mixtec Indian who has managed to eke out a good living from the generosity of the gringos. When they are visiting, she is the humblest and saddest Christian woman, cooing things like "I am God's poorest little child" to the translators. When they're gone, she likes her *mezcal* and her cigars, becomes a tyrant, and uses her imagined position of power to coerce and threaten the neighbors into doing her bidding.

Her latest ploy is to convert her small barn into a church, which various evangelical groups use for services and Bible studies. Each group pays Josefina, if not in money, in clothes and food and soda cans and prestige. The current gossip about her is that she is a Satanist and that she works black magic on her enemies. Cuquis whispers to Juanita that

Josefina has sacrificed a baby. Someone or other saw it, it's true.

"I heard," Juanita says, "that she has sex with the Devil."

Cuquis and Perla look at each other and nod: there is no doubt about it.

Perla makes the sign of the cross, lest Josefina give her the evil eye—*el mal de ojo*—and somehow harm the baby within her. Babies have been born with horns, tails. Everyone knows it's true. She shudders, even though the sun has already burned the hilltop into the high eighties.

"Old witch," she mutters.

Josefina has a different take on the situation. She can remember when she gave birth in that same little barn they use for church. She was alone, no one there even to hold her hand. And she remembers cutting the umbilical cord herself, with a kitchen knife. And she remembers almost losing that same baby to a terrible pox that the missionaries cured with an injection and cans of fluid that she threw away because the color looked evil to her.

She remembers her mother being kicked in the stomach by Mexicans just like these women. Why shouldn't she have something extra? Nobody but her takes in abandoned Indian children. She even feeds orphaned *mestizo* kids, though she doesn't love anyone outside her tribe. Except the missionaries. She loves them quite a bit. Her favorites are the Baptists, though she is Catholic. The Baptists have the best doughnuts.

Josefina has her own family to feed plus three new orphan boys. Let them talk all they want. None of them had the strength of will to force their husbands to build a barn. You keep a man too busy to do mischief, and you have to be stronger than him. Take control and keep them scrambling—anybody knew that much.

And as long as the gringos don't know that she has the biggest pigpens in the area—hidden down the back side of the hill—they will take pity on her. For the situation in Mexico has reduced urban Mixteca women to one thing: begging. They stand in traffic in every big Mexican city, and if they are lucky, they have a baby at their breast. Their greatest art, now that their pyramids are gone and forgotten and their cities laid to waste and overgrown with weeds and jungles, is pity. Everything depends on how abject they can look, how piping and pitiable their voices, how huge their eyes. How much of their breast is revealed as the baby suckles. The tribal women, called Marias by the Mexicans, have learned to massage the appalling sentimentality of gringos and *mestizos*. While the modern world grinds them like corn, its operators occasionally feel saddened by the big black eyes and toss out a few cents. Josefina is only doing what Mexico has told her she must do. She begs. But she will not grovel. Let the missionaries fill her gut and cover her back. Let the women of the barrio fear her.

She says to her friends, Why shouldn't I have power over these damned Mexicans?

When no one is listening, she sings songs in her own tongue.

One P.M.

Boys shuffle off to Josefina's barn. There, men have set up curtained shower stalls made from galvanized tubs and PVC piping. The girls wander down the road to a small house with a real floor. Astonishingly robust Baptist women stomp around making loud noises and wide gestures. The Mexican and Indian women surreptitiously gawk at these golden beings, wondering how they get so shiny, how they manage to stay clean and get so tall. Their eyes are often blue, their skin peachy and smooth. You can smell them from a meter away: perfume, deodorant, mint chewing gum, shampoos and conditioners and whatever other lotions they have smeared on themselves. None of them smell like pee, sweat, or bad teeth. Their breasts are pointy and as hard as fruit, it's obvious. They have big solid asses, and they all seem to love Jesus, even when they don't always give evidence of loving the poor. The neighbors think the gringo men are often cute, if a little soft. But these gringas. It's like a television set has broken open and these bellowing female giants have stormed out among real people. Every woman in line is happy that their men are away, at work. And Juanita is keeping her eye open for her favorite, the pastor.

Fifty-one other women watch for him too.

One-thirty P.M.

The children are shampooed first. They line up and dip their heads into tubs as more *americanos* splash water and shampoo on them. Many of the kids have lice, so there is a lot of Kwell lice-killing shampoo in the water. Many mothers don't want their children to be washed here, because it doesn't take long for the tub to look like it's full of Nestlé's Quik, chocolate and thick and floating with dying lice. Babies scream and kick. And the young Bible student volunteers laugh and sparkle and curse in the weirdly gutted fashion of evangelicals: Gosh! Dang! Gosh darn it! Darn you! Oh good gosh!

After the shampoo, it's off to the baths. And after the baths, the children receive their treats. Each gets a bag with two doughnuts, two or three pieces of fruit, and a carton of cold chocolate milk the color of their bathwater. They have each earned a few points, paid in poker chips and rubber stamps on the backs of their hands. With these points, they can purchase candy, or popcorn, or even small toys and toothbrushes, at the *bodega* set up in one of the vans.

For most of the mothers, these afternoons are the only times they have freedom. Their men are gone, and someone else is caring for their children. They gather and gossip, flirt, show off, fight. They line up at various vans to receive their goods. After they have gone through the line, they run to the end and hope there is enough left for seconds. Sly women send their children into other lines, and they switch places, sometimes sending family members through three or four times. These are the venture capitalists of the neighborhood.

Hermana Josefina outrages them all by refusing to enter any line. She stands near the door of her barn and smiles at them like some benign queen vaguely amused by their antics. She makes a great show of hugging the pastor as he tries to enter the barn. Her skin is almost black against his grizzled white arms. Her eyes, peeking around him and flashing at the women in the lines, are as impenetrable as obsidian.

Cuquis nudges Juanita.

"That old witch is stealing your man."

The other women laugh.

Juana ignores them and turns to Perla.

"Little Mother," she says. "What about Braulio?"

"What about him?"

"Well? What about him?"

"Braulio?"

"Yes."

"Our Braulio?"

"He's the only Braulio I know."

"Oh," Perla says, looking off. "He's not horrible."

"Do you like him?"

"I don't like being alone."

"But do you like *him?*"

"Maybe."

"Think about him," Juanita says. "I like him for you."

"Braulio," Perla repeats.

Cuquis looks at her and grins.

"What's your problem?" Perla snaps.

Cuquis can read. She pores over a Bible the missionaries have given her. "Listen to this," she says. " 'Let the rich man glory in his humiliation, because like flowering grass he will pass away. For the sun rises with a scorching wind and withers the grass. And its flower falls off. And the beauty of its appearance is destroyed. So too the rich man in his pursuits will fade away.' "

Several of the women mutter, "Amen."

"Good old Jesus Christ," Cuca says. "He'll kick the shit out of those rich bastards."

One forty-five P.M.

The van doors swing open. The women surge, almost break out of line and rush ahead in a little riot, but they already know that at the first sign of pandemonium, the doors will close and the food will drive away. Two weeks without provisions. So they shove each other and jostle a bit and hiss and tsk and mutter, but they hold formation.

They each receive:

> One kilo of pinto beans, weighed and poured into a
>   brown paper lunch bag
> Six potatoes
> Three onions
> One kilo of long-grain rice, also poured into a
>   brown paper bag
> A few apples or oranges or bananas.

They are in luck today! The next van has canned food. It's a strange mixture, and some of it will have to go to the pigs because nobody knows what to do with it.

Veg-All. Creamed corn. Pear halves. Pumpkin pie filling. Pickled beets. Spam. Corned beef hash. Beefaroni. Tuna. Sauerkraut. Carnation condensed milk. Smoked oysters. Something without a label, flecked with rust. Alpo.

"What's this?" says Perla, holding up a small can. It says *Escargots.*

"Look at the picture," says Juanita.

Perla makes a face.

"The picture has snails on it."

Juanita grabs the can and stares at it.

"My God," she says. "Gringos eat bugs."

"I'm going to barf," Perla says.

They throw the can away.

Three-thirty P.M.

The pastor has felt guilty for years, watching the women stand in these ragged lines, waiting. He wants to make them happy, not just to feed them or preach to them. It has recently occurred to him to give them a carnival. He has invested some money and a lot of time in creating a series of midway games for the mothers to enjoy—*competencias*, they call them. There is a balance beam and a beanbag toss, pitching games and even a game with ray guns and bleeping flashing targets. The women compete for candy bars and Cokes. They have grown to love the games, and they hurry from the food lines to line up and take aim with their three beanbags.

Juanita waits for the pastor to come out of the bathing room. When he finally does step out, in a hurry as always, she feels a thrill. He is the tallest man she has ever hugged, and she throws her arms around him before he can get away. He can't speak a lick of Spanish, and he does his best, patting her on the back and saying, "*¡Ah! ¡Sí, sí! ¡Hola! ¡Muy bien!*" as he tries to escape her grip. He has two more orphanages to get to today, and they're running a half-hour late as it is.

"Hermano," she says as he pulls away. "Hermana Consuelo is hurt."

The pastor waits for the translator to repeat it, then he asks, "How hurt?"

"*Cabeza*," says Juanita, indicating the head. "*Mucha sangre.*"

The pastor understands this perfectly well. He has seen a swimming pool's worth of *sangre* these last thirty years.

"*Muy mal*," Juanita says. "*Está en su cama.*"

"She's in bed," the translator says, sounding like a monkey to Juanita. "Real bad."

The pastor looks at his watch, sighs, says, "Let's go take a look."

Juanita is thrilled when he puts an arm lightly on her shoulders as they pass the lines of neighbors and sharks. She looks back at Cuquis and Perla and scrunches her nose at them, wiggles her hips. The pastor is oblivious: he's wondering when the hell he'll get a chance to eat something.

In the doorway behind them, Josefina is fuming.

Four P.M.

They collect Braulio as they walk. The pastor likes Braulio—he can see a good heart in him. "Broolio," he says, the translator behind him like an echo, "you're a winner. You're a special boy." Braulio blushes. It's like God sticking a gold star on your homework.

Homework.

"Pastor," he blurts, "I want to go back to school!"

The pastor smiles.

"Well, let me see what I can do about that."

Braulio can't believe his ears.

"*Gracias,*" he says.

"*¡Ah! ¡Sí! ¡Bueno, bueno!*" the pastor enthuses.

They knock at Hermana Consuelo's doorway. They can hear her old husband, Pepe, blind and *muy loco*, shuffling around inside.

"*Mamá, Mamá,*" he is saying. "*¿ 'onde 'stá Mamá?*"

They step in, and Braulio's mouth drops open. He moves behind the pastor and hides. Juanita touches the pastor's arm and then crosses herself. It takes them a second to figure out what they see, but in the cramped gloom of the shack, the terrible scene reveals itself: blind Pepe, immensely fat and shirtless, is tied by the wrist to the center pole that holds up the roof. The rope has cut into his skin, and he has walked around and around the pole, like a tied dog, until he has come up tight against the pole and can't move.

"Where's Mamá?" he asks. "Where's Mamá?"

Hermana Consuelo is lying on her back on their nearly black mattress, dead. Her mouth is open, full of congealed blood. Blood has run from her nostrils, forming a black mustache. Her eyes stare. Flies hurry along her lips, pausing occasionally to scrub their hands. Braulio doesn't want to cry, but he bursts into tears anyway, and Juanita takes him against her breast, where he sobs.

The pastor covers Consuelo's face with her blanket and takes out his knife and cuts Don Pepe loose.

He lightly embraces Juanita and Braulio and says, "Let's step outside now and leave her alone."

The translator forgets to say anything.

Five P.M.

The gringos are gone.

The pastor has given Braulio a ride over to the dump to

collect Don Manuel. Nobody knows what to do, but Manuel and Lalo will think of something. The pastor has left $100 with Josefina to help pay for the burial. "Fina!" Juanita snaps. "She'll steal the money!"

As the gringos drive away, and as Perla, against all orders, steps inside to look at Consuelo's body and Juanita and Cuquis lead poor crazy Don Pepe to Juanita's house, one of Fina's nieces breaks away from the crowd to tell her what Juanita has been saying about her.

Braulio wades through the trash, looking for Manuel. He finally spots him by a stack of bulging bags. Manuel has pulled off his gloves, and he's drinking water from a plastic jug, waiting for Lalo to come collect him and take him home.

"Uncle!" Braulio calls.

Manuel looks over at him and waves for him to come closer.

"What brings you to the *dompe?*" Manuel asks.

"Doña Consuelo!" Braulio cries. "She died!"

"What do you mean, she died?"

"She's dead. All full of blood. Her mouth and nose."

Manuel whistles.

Braulio says, "She drowned in her own blood, it looks like! I thought I was going to be sick!"

Manuel hands him the water jug, and Braulio takes a drink. Manuel puts his hand on Braulio's shoulder and says, "Now listen. When Lalo comes, you don't say anything. I'll tell him. You keep quiet. All right?"

Braulio nods.

"Not a word," Manuel says.

"No."

They wait.

Soon Lalo comes banging along the dirt track that runs

alongside the dump. He waves out the window at them. He parks and gets out.

"Another no-good long goddamned day," he says, smiling his wild pirate's smile.

"Lalo," Manuel says. "Come here for a minute."

He leads Lalo off to the side, puts his arm around his shoulders, and puts his face near his *compadre*'s. Lalo pulls away. "What!" Braulio hears him shout. Then Manuel speaks to him some more. Lalo puts his hand over his eyes. He lowers himself to the ground and sits with his head hanging and his eyes covered. When Manuel says something else to him, he swings his arm blindly, throwing a wild punch that rakes in only air. Silently, Manuel sits beside his friend and looks at the tractors making their way out of the clouds of seagulls.

Seven P.M.

All Lalo could say when he got home was "I'm sorry. I'm sorry." They all told him it wasn't his fault, but he feels the guilt crushing him. And he has begun to wrestle with the debt he now owes. Must he now care for Don Pepe? Can he care for the old madman? He knows the least he can do is build Consuelo a coffin. He is afraid to see her, afraid to face what his carelessness has done, for he is a man of conscience, and he knows his impatience killed her. "Don't make me look at her," he begged Manuel. "I can't. I can't."

Later, he knows, he will be drunk. Very, very drunk. But not yet. He has work to do. Manuel has taken him off to buy wood. It's the least he can do.

Consuelo's house is dark. Lit candles sputter before her door, and several women, led by Cuquis, say a rosary outside. Their quiet voices sound like muffled music. Juanita's house is bright. Lit up, with the door open. Everyone in the barrio has been coming around to leave money with her. Most of them give Don Pepe a hug. He chuckles; he thinks it's his birthday or Christmas. "Oh!" he cries with each hug. "Hello! Hello!"

Juanita collects the sums in a coffee can, and Perla carefully scratches each person's name on a piece of notebook paper. Braulio sits across from her and watches.

"What are you looking at?" she says.

"You," he replies.

"Why?"

"You're beautiful."

She puts down her pencil and looks at him for a long while.

Juanita has tied Don Pepe to a chair. She spoon-feeds him warm creamed corn. He smacks his lips. The children are terrified of him. Huevona peers out from behind the cloth bedroom door, wide-eyed. She smells like Ivory soap and baby shampoo. She hates smelling so sweet.

Don Pepe smells like wet cigars.

Juanita calls to her.

"You, Huevona! Come here."

She steps into the room, cutting a wide detour around smelly Don Pepe.

"Where's Mama?" he asks the blank air.

"The pastor gave that witch Fina one hundred dollars to help pay for the funeral."

Huevona nods her head, wide-eyed. She always looks like a deer, or a wildcat.

"Go up there and collect it for me," Juanita says. "Tell her we have all the burial money here, and we are keeping a record of who pays so we can show the pastor we did our part."

Huevona nods.

"Do you understand?"

Huevona nods again.

"Then get going!" Juanita claps her hands. Huevona

jumps. She takes Braulio's hand and tugs. He resists for a second.

"Don't worry," Juanita says. "La Perla will still be here when you come back."

Both Braulio and Perla blush.

When he steps out with the little girl, everyone, even crazy Don Pepe, is laughing.

Across town, Lalo and Manuel are working in Lalo's cousin's yard. They have several planks of raw pine between them, and they are cutting them up with a borrowed saw. Though they are still horrified over Consuelo's death, they are also getting the giggles. Lalo's cousin has poured two beers down their throats already, and he has gone to get some tequila.

"Goddamn it, Lalo," Manuel says. "Did you have to kill her tonight? I was going to make love to Juanita!"

Lalo falls down laughing.

"Stop it! You're killing me!"

"Look who's talking," Manuel says.

Juanita looks up as fat Mari stops by.

"I only have fifty cents," Mari says, "but I brought something for Don Pepe."

"*Mamá?*" Don Pepe asks, his poached-looking eyes rolling back and forth.

"No, old man, it's me, Marilu." She kisses him on the head. "I brought you some candy."

"Oh!" He laughs. "Candy!"

She unwraps a Tootsie Roll Pop and puts it in his mouth. He sucks it like a baby.

"Mari," Perla says as she writes down *Marilu, cincuenta centavos*. "Gringos eat bugs."

"You don't say."

"It's true! We saw a can of snails this afternoon."

"*Dios mío*," Mari says. "Leave it to gringos to cook snails."

All the women pause to shake their heads.

Eight-thirty P.M.

Abandoned, the coffin lies half finished. Lalo is asleep. Manuel and Lalo's cousin are drunk and singing love songs. Tears run down Manuel's cheeks. It does not occur to him to go home. He takes the bottle. The tequila rips down his throat like a bare electric wire. "I don't give a shit," he says to no one, no one at all.

Nine P.M.

Braulio and Huevona slink into the house. Juanita sees them and turns in her chair. Josefina is standing in the doorway, smoking a cigar. She blows smoke into the room. They can smell her: she's been drinking.

"Fina," Juanita says, nodding. "Come in."

Josefina stands there, unmoving. Smoke leaks out of her nostrils like something alive and greasy. It crawls up her face and over her hair.

Perla coughs.

"The smoke bothers me," she says.

"Don't talk back to me, *morra*," Josefina says.

Perla, never one to pass up a fight, says, "How can I talk back when you haven't said anything?"

Josefina takes one step forward.

"Do you need to learn some manners?" she asks.

Braulio rises and extends his hands, making peace.

"*No hay pedo*," he says, the absurd lower-class slang for "There's no trouble here," which can only be translated as "There is no fart between us." "*Calma.*"

Juanita watches, tense, ready to jump.

Don Pepe is asleep, his sad rocky head hanging, drool falling onto his chest.

"Fina," Juanita says. "Did you bring the money?"

"Money," Fina says, and turns her deadly red eyes toward Juana. "Money. I hear you think I'm a thief."

Juana casts her eyes down.

"I hear," Fina says, rolling the cigar in her mouth, smelling of ferment and fire, "you think I'm a witch."

Braulio steps toward her and makes the mistake of touching her arm.

"Fina—" he manages to say before she shocks him with a right-handed roundhouse slap that knocks him off his feet.

Inside Juanita's house, it looks like there has been an explosion.

Braulio falls.

Huevona screams and runs.

The other children scream and scatter.

The little dog bursts out from under the table, barking.

The table tips over.

Piglets fly like shrapnel.

Juanita flies out of her seat and strikes Fina.

Perla, shrieking like a cat, throws herself over Braulio, who is crawling across the floor, and tackles both women.

They hit the floor in an avalanche of chairs and plates and forks and billowing skirts.

Pepe wakes up with a start and cries out, "Mamá! Where is Mamá!"

Screams, grunts, smacks, curses, crashes, shatterings, thuds, snarls.

Pepe tries to get up, still tied to the chair, yelling for Mama to come get him, and the women roll into him and knock him over backward.

Braulio staggers to his feet, turns the wrong way, and plunges through one of the paper walls.

Manuel's framed military diploma falls and the glass breaks.

Juanita has Fina by the hair, and she is punching her in the face. Punching, punching, hammering.

Fina throws a kick that catches Perla in her huge pregnant stomach, and Perla staggers back, clutching herself, almost retching, and she hits the Coleman stove, and the boiling pot of rice flies to the floor, scalding everyone, and the gas-feed line breaks, and a terrible hissing escapes, and flames billow high, scrabbling up the wall.

They all pause for the slightest moment, listening to this strange sound, before they try to run out the door.

Yelling for the children.

Perla screaming, "Braulio!"

And Braulio steps back into the room as the gas bottle explodes and blows him backward, right out through the wall of the bedroom.

Nine-thirty P.M.

Everyone stands and watches Juana's house burn. One of the piglets is trapped inside and is screeching as it burns. Perla holds her hands over her ears. Braulio tries to hug her and all the children at once. Everyone is weeping. Fina, blood on her face, sheepishly comforts Juanita.

"I'm sorry," she says, made sober by the fire. "Want a cigar?"

Juana counts heads—everyone is accounted for except for Manuel and the pot-head couple. Well, they're all off drunk somewhere, and thank God for that.

The firemen don't get there until ten-thirty. Someone has had to run a half-mile to the phone booth beside the general store. The firemen are contacted, but it takes quite a while to explain where the fire is. The firemen have had to traverse downtown Tijuana, then rush south on a two-lane road.

They've been driving around the hills, trying to discover the dirt road up here, and by the time they arrive, the fire has almost burned itself out. It gutters and smolders, but it's down to the ground. They hardly have to spray any water on it at all.

"Perla," Juana says. "Did you save the money?"

Perla holds up the coffee can.

"*Gracias a Dios*," Juana says.

Don Pepe sits in the dirt, sucking his Tootsie Roll Pop.

Everything is gone.

Midnight.

The neighbors return now, each carrying a small item to give to Juanita: an undershirt for Manuel when he gets home, a bag of powdered doughnuts, a blanket, a pillow, three eggs, a battered old pot, a cigarette, a bottle of rum, a coat, a potato, wet panties just washed and wrung out.

"They're almost new," the woman says to Juana. "They have flowers on them."

Juana hugs her. Juana hugs many people. Some of them have only hugs to offer.

Cuquis and the funeral prayer circle have moved nearer to Juana's clan, and they now pray for them.

Juanita is too tired to cry.

Braulio and Fina have gone to Fina's barn and collected a heavy sheet of plastic. Braulio has an idea. Fina's sons help him haul the sheet back to Juana's yard. Everything stinks of smoke. Everything and everybody is black.

"Glory to God," Juana repeats often. "We are all safe. Everybody's all right."

"At least we're together, Mama," Perla says.

"Glory to God. Glory to God."

Braulio has seen that the wooden frame he moved away from the house is safe, unburned in the far corner. He drags it forward, around the glowing embers of the house, and he says, "I can build us a tent."

Amazed, Juanita and Perla watch Braulio take charge of all the men who stand around gawking.

"All right, you lazy bastards," he says, sounding exactly like Manuel, "we have work to do."

And they get to work.

Two A.M.

The children are asleep in an unruly pile on the clothes that the neighbors have brought. Cuquis has taken poor old Don Pepe home with her. He will escape while she sleeps, however, and will be discovered without his pants in the morning, wandering around the basketball court. The moon can be seen through the clear plastic lean-to Braulio has constructed. He looks over at Juanita: she sleeps in the dirt, her head on the one pillow. In her hand is the charred corner of Manuel's diploma.

Carefully, trying to make no sound, he scoots over closer to Perla. She sleeps on her side, with her knees drawn up, and one hand covers her mouth. He stares at her in the gloom. He cries, looking at her. He longs to put his mouth on her mouth and to feel her hot breath inside his mouth. He imagines it tastes sweet. He wants to take her heavy hair in his hands and squeeze it.

He thinks, as he often thinks, if she will just marry him, he will show her what kind of a man he is. Or can be, anyway. He is only fourteen. Perla is thirteen.

Braulio's transistor radio is murmuring softly beside them.

That *conjunto pop* from Mexico City, Maná, is singing. They say, "You are my religion."

He'll build her the dream house.

He'll work every day.

He'll get her a television.

And a pig.

He'll make new babies inside her.

He'll plant flowers in their yard.

He'll die for her.

He moves close to her, carefully, carefully—his jaws ache with the tension. And he maneuvers himself under her tattered blanket, wanting to feel her heat as she sleeps. Wanting to be near her. He can't stop crying. He stretches himself out on the ground beside her and closes his eyes. He can smell her sweat. He leans close and lightly lets his lips touch her hair.

He is startled when her hand reaches out and clasps his.

Silently she pulls his fingers toward her belly, moves them up and down on the taut softness of it. Then she moves his hand up to her breast and cups herself with his hand and snuggles in against him and goes back to sleep.

Braulio lies awake, stiff, afraid to move, afraid to breathe.

All he can think to do is pray.

Five A.M., and snuffling and snoring fills the tent.

Doña Juana wakes first, and for a brief moment she can't remember what happened. She sits up and is startled to see the ruins, the tent, the children tucked in around her. She is also startled to see Perla caught up in Braulio's arms and their legs tangled together. She looks up and sees a burly shadow through the plastic. She crawls out and looks into Manuel's eyes.

"Are you all right?" he asks.

"We're all safe," she says.

Manuel hangs his head.

She goes to him.

"There is nothing you could have done, *viejo*."

"I'm sorry, is all," he replies, taking her in his arms. "I'm sorry."

Lalo is keeping his distance.

He is ready to help, but he is not sure what is to be done.

"I saved this for you," Juana says, handing Manuel the corner of the diploma. "Everything else is gone."

"Everything."

"Everything."

Manuel turns to Lalo and says, "Everything is gone."

"Everything?"

"Everything."

"*Chingue a su madre*," Lalo says.

Juana says, "Braulio has some good ideas."

"Braulio!"

"He was the hero. He took charge. And he has ideas for a new house."

"Braulio," Manuel says. "Imagine that."

"He's a philosopher," Lalo calls. "Smart."

Juana says, "He's going to be your son-in-law, I think."

Manuel throws his hands in the air.

"Did anything *not* happen while I was gone?" he cries.

"Jesus Christ didn't return, looks like," Lalo says.

Manuel glares at him.

"Come," Juanita says to her man. "Rest with me."

"I can't rest!" Manuel says. "Look at this! Our lives are gone."

"No, *viejo*, our lives are here." She puts her hand on his chest. "Our lives are here, no? Our things are gone, that's all."

"Yeah," says Lalo. "You didn't have anything anyway. Screw it."

Manuel just looks at him.

Lalo shrugs.

"You know. Another *pinche* day of life, *compadre*," he offers. Then he walks to his own house.

Manuel nudges Juana. She looks up at him.

"I brought you a flower," he says.

He pulls a battered rose out of his pocket.

"Oh, you," she says, taking it and holding it to her chest. "My little old man."

They hold each other and weep softly, looking over the smoking gray and black charcoal pit that was their house. Juana pulls him tight and rocks him back and forth. She speaks into his chest, so he doesn't hear her at first. She has to repeat herself. She says, "Next time we build a house, let's plant a garden. Let's plant roses." She's thinking of Braulio, of his dreams and his ideas. She smiles into Manuel's ribs. "Roses," she says. "They're like music for your eyes."

And Manuel closes his eyes for a moment and listens: small birds are singing all over the hill. Where do they hide, all the little birds? Why don't they fly across the border, where the gringos probably throw food all over the streets? So many songs in the cool air—so many tiny, insistent, hopeful voices.

"These birds, I think," he says, "all speak Spanish."

"What are they saying?" she murmurs.

"They're saying, 'Hey—at least it's not raining.' "